Lesson 1.14 Conjunctions

||| || |||||| || ||||| ||| |||||||||| |||
↻ **W9-APT-129**

Identify It

Identify the conjunctions in the following sentences as coordinate, correlative, or subordinate. Write **CD** for coordinate, **CR** for correlative, or **S** for subordinate after each sentence.

1. _____ Are we going to go biking or hiking on Saturday?

2. _____ Neither pasta nor pizza was offered on the menu.

3. _____ As long as it's raining, we may as well get our homework done.

4. _____ Either Rachel or Carrie will be voted president of the class.

5. _____ Let's walk to school since it is a sunny, warm day.

6. _____ Todd wants to play baseball this weekend but he has a class in the morning.

7. _____ While we are waiting in line, let's get some popcorn.

8. _____ Both the girls' and the boys' teams are going to the championship.

9. _____ Grant wants mushrooms and peppers on his pizza.

10. _____ After this week, there's only six weeks of school this year.

Try It

Write five sentences of your own using the conjunctions. Use two conjunctions from each category.

1. _____

   _____

2. _____

   _____

3. _____

   _____

4. _____

   _____

5. _____

   _____

Lesson 1.15 Interjections

An **interjection** is a one- or two-word phrase used to express surprise or strong emotion.

Common interjections:

Ah	Hurray
Aha	Oh
Alas	Ouch
Aw	Uh
Cheers	Uh-huh
Eh	Uh-uh
Hey	Well
Hi	Wow
Huh	Yeah

An exclamation mark is usually used after an interjection to separate it from the rest of the sentence.

Oh! I'm so happy that you can make the trip!

If the feeling isn't quite as strong, a comma is used in place of the exclamation point.

Oh, that's too bad he won't be joining us.

Sometimes question marks are used as an interjection's punctuation.

Eh? Is that really true?

Find It

Use a dictionary to look up each of the following interjections. Write the word's part of speech and the dictionary definition. Then, use each interjection in a sentence.

1. ah - _____

   _____

2. alas - _____

   _____

3. eh - _____

   _____

4. hey - _____

   _____

5. oh - _____

   _____

6. ouch - _____

   _____

Lesson 1.17 Articles

Proof It
Proofread the following paragraph. Look for mistakes in the use of articles. Use the proof marks to delete incorrect words and insert the correct words.

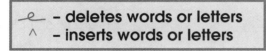

- *e* – deletes words or letters
- ^ – inserts words or letters

You've probably read much about the White House, a Washington Memorial, and an Lincoln Memorial in Washington, D.C. But how much do you know about a U.S. Capitol Building? The U.S. Capitol is not just an building in Washington, D.C. It is symbolically and architecturally important. It also has practical significance. The U.S. Capitol is the home of a House of Representatives and the Senate. If visiting Washington, D.C., an dome at the east end of an National Mall on Capitol Hill gives the U.S. Capitol away. The U.S. Capitol is also considered to be the museum. Inside, a eager visitor can find many examples of American art and history. The U.S. Capitol is an symbol of American government.

Try It
Write a paragraph with five sentences about a local landmark. Once you have finished your paragraph, underline the articles.

_____

_____

_____

_____

_____

_____

_____

_____

_____

_____

Review Chapter 1 Lessons 12–17

Review: Adjectives, Adverbs

Read each sentence below. When you see **(adj.)**, fill in the blank with an adjective. When you see **(adv.)**, fill in the blank with an adverb.

1. The twins (adv.) _____ crept up the stairs.

2. As the children watched, the (adj.) _____ panda sat down to munch on a stalk of bamboo.

3. Isaiah took a bite of the (adj.) _____ soup.

4. The crowd cheered (adv.) _____ in the stands.

5. Clementine plucked (adj.) _____ apples from the trees in the orchard.

6. Both my brothers (adv.) _____ agreed to clean their room in exchange for their allowances.

7. The (adj.) _____ waves soothed Jack's sunburn.

8. Make sure you drive (adv.) _____ on the frozen roads!

Review: Coordinate Conjunctions, Correlative Conjunctions, Subordinate Conjunctions

Circle the conjunction in each sentence. On the line, write whether it is a coordinate, correlative, or subordinate conjunction.

1. The dragonfly and the bumblebee circled the flower. _____

2. Neither Eddie nor Dante has been sick at all this summer. _____

3. Since Tasha has moved to Oregon, I have not had a best friend. _____

4. Both Chestnut and Blaze like to spend the day in the pasture. _____

5. While her mom is at the library, Minh will play at the park. _____

6. Irina wants to go to the play, but Ivan hopes to see a movie. _____

Review   Chapter 1 Lessons 12–17

Review: Adjectives, Adverbs, Conjunctions, Interjections, Prepositions, Articles

In each sentence, circle the preposition or prepositions. Underline the object of each preposition.

1. Can you imagine living in the Arctic and hunting for mussels under a layer of ice?

2. At low tide, an Inuit might carve a hole in the ocean ice.

3. He can walk along the ocean floor.

4. A thick layer of ice lies above his head.

5. The mussels burrow below the sand.

6. The Inuit man places them inside his bucket.

7. The sound of rushing water is not far.

8. He must hurry back before the icy water surrounds him.

Review: Adjectives, Adverbs, Conjunctions, Interjections, Prepositions, Articles

Write the part of speech above the words in bold. Write **ADJ** for adjectives, **ADV** for adverbs, **CONJ** for conjunctions, **INT** for interjections, **PREP** for prepositions, and **ART** for articles.

Hurray! Happy Birthday!

Birthdays were **first** celebrated **in ancient** Rome. **The** Romans celebrated **the** birthdays **of** their **favorite** gods **and important** people, like **the** emperor. **In** Britain, they celebrate **the Queen's** birthday. **In the** United States, **the** birthdays **of** presidents **and important** leaders, like Martin Luther King, are celebrated. **In** Japan, Korea, **and** China, the **sixtieth** birthday marks a transition **from an active** life **to** one **of** contemplation. **Many Eastern** cultures don't even recognize **the actual** date **of** birth. When **the first** moon **of the new** year arrives, everyone is **one year** older.

Lesson 1.18 Declarative Sentences

Declarative sentences are sentences that make statements. They say something about a place, person, thing, or idea. When punctuating a declarative sentence, use a period at the end of the sentence.

> Henry Bergh was the founder of the American Society for the Prevention of Cruelty to Animals.
>
> Pizza is my favorite food.
>
> Marathons are 26.2 miles long.

Identify It

Place a check mark in front of each declarative sentence. Leave the other sentences blank.

1. _____ Venice is a city in Italy.

2. _____ Venice has a network of canals used for transportation.

3. _____ Have you ever been to Venice?

4. _____ The Grand Canal is the main thoroughfare.

5. _____ Three bridges cross the Grand Canal.

6. _____ How many bridges cross the Grand Canal?

7. _____ Look at the beautiful bridge!

8. _____ Venice has a very temperate climate.

9. _____ How warm does it get in Venice in the summer?

10. _____ Venice is one of the most beautiful cities in Europe.

Lesson 1.18 Declarative Sentences

Proof It

Make sure that each declarative sentence ends in a period. If the punctuation is correct, place a check mark before the sentence. If not, use the proofreading marks to make each declarative sentence end with a period.

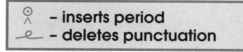

> ⊙ – **inserts period**
> ∧
> ℓ – **deletes punctuation**

1. _____ I want to play baseball tomorrow.

2. _____ I can't wait to go to the gym with Greg and Sarah?

3. _____ If you order pizza, make sure to get onions.

4. _____ Do you see the rainbow?

5. _____ Jen said that it is time to eat?

Try It

Write a dialogue between two people. Write ten sentences about a place they are visiting. Be sure to use periods when you are making declarative sentences.

_____

_____

_____

_____

_____

_____

_____

_____

_____

_____

_____

_____

_____

_____

_____

_____

Lesson 1.19 Interrogative Sentences

Interrogative sentences are sentences that ask questions. When punctuating an interrogative sentence, use a question mark.

  Did I see lightning in the sky**?**
  Do you like fresh spinach in your salad**?**
  Do you run in the morning or in the evening**?**

Complete It

Complete the following sentences by circling the correct punctuation.

1. Alla walked briskly five times around the block (. ?)

2. Did you see the famous statue on your vacation (. ?)

3. The spider spun a beautiful web (. ?)

4. Did the poem inspire your artwork (. ?)

5. How quickly did you complete the obstacle course (. ?)

6. The designer showed great style (. ?)

7. I like the rhythm of that song (. ?)

8. Did your dad make spaghetti for dinner last night (. ?)

9. Are you going to try out for the wrestling team (. ?)

10. Do you lift weights to strengthen your muscles (. ?)

11. Are those chestnuts I smell roasting (. ?)

12. My friends are coming over after dinner (. ?)

13. I think the batteries are dead in that radio (. ?)

14. Aren't the pictures in the museum beautiful (. ?)

15. Where are you going after school (. ?)

16. Who is at the door (. ?)

17. Jon and I walked around the block (. ?)

18. The baseball game starts at seven o'clock tonight (. ?)

19. What time did you say (. ?)

20. Arlene and Beth joined a book club (. ?)

Lesson 1.19 Interrogative Sentences

Solve It

A farmer is taking a student on a tour of his garden. The student has many questions about what kind of vegetables he grows. The farmer's answers are given, but the student's questions are missing. Write the question with the appropriate punctuation in the space provided. The first one has been done for you.

1. How many vegetables do you grow?   I grow many vegetables.

2. _____   I grow mostly soy beans.

3. _____   My favorite vegetable is broccoli.

4. _____   If you want to be a farmer, you should study many subjects, but especially science, math, and social studies.

Try It

Write a list of questions you might ask a local business owner.

_____

_____

_____

_____

_____

_____

_____

_____

_____

_____

_____

Lesson 1.20 Exclamatory Sentences

Exclamatory sentences are sentences that reveal urgency, strong surprise, or emotion. When punctuating an exclamatory sentence, use an exclamation mark.

I can't believe you ate the whole pie!
Look at how much weight he is lifting!
I think I smell a skunk!

Only use exclamation points when expressing urgency and strong surprise or emotion. Exclamation marks can also be used in dialogue, when the character or speaker is making an urgent or emotional statement.

Identify It
Identify which sentences are exclamatory by putting an exclamation mark at the end of the sentences. If it's not exclamatory, leave it blank.

1. Watch out for the ice

2. Ouch! I can't believe I stubbed my toe on the table again

3. Where are you having dinner tonight

4. The storm is quickly coming our way

5. I'm not sure if I want to go to the movies or not

6. It is so cold I think I have frostbite

7. Don't you like the cold weather

8. Ah! The sunset is gorgeous

9. You're it

10. Oh no! The bridge is out

11. What time is it

12. Oranges are my favorite fruit

13. Watch out! The oranges fell off the display

14. The Lord of the Rings is my favorite series of books

15. That author really inspires me

Lesson 1.20 Exclamatory Sentences

Rewrite It

Read the following postcard from one friend to another. The writer seems excited about her trip, but doesn't express it in her writing. Rewrite the postcard changing declarative sentences to exclamatory ones.

Dear Linda,

I'm having a wonderful time in Florida. The weather is fantastic. It's been sunny every day. We went swimming in the hotel's pool on Tuesday. Then, on Wednesday, we actually swam in the ocean. Tomorrow we are going to visit a marine animal sanctuary. Do you remember studying about the rescued marine animals in school? I can't wait to see the fish and animals. I wish you were here. See you soon.

Drew

_____

_____

_____

_____

_____

_____

Try It

Write a postcard to a friend or relative about a trip you have taken recently. Make it exciting by including exclamatory sentences. Make sentences exclamatory when you really want them to stand out.

_____

_____

_____

_____

_____

_____

Lesson 1.21 Imperative Sentences

Imperative sentences demand that an action be performed. The subjects of imperative sentences are usually not expressed. They usually contain the understood subject *you*. Imperative sentences can be punctuated with a period or an exclamation mark. Use an exclamation mark in the same instances as you would for an exclamatory sentence, such as expressing urgency, surprise, or strong emotion.

Look at the rabbit behind the trees.
(*You* look at the rabbit behind the trees.)

Write the note here.
(*You* write the note here.)

Throw me the ball!
(*You* throw me the ball!)

Complete It

Choose a verb from the box that will complete each imperative sentence and write it on the line provided. Remember, the subject *you* is implied in the sentences.

carry	drive	pick	swing	vote
drink	pass	shoot	throw	yell

1. _____ for Simon for president!

2. _____ the potatoes, please.

3. _____ up the paper from the floor.

4. _____ that bag for your aunt.

5. _____ the ball to second base!

6. _____ slowly when on ice.

7. _____ the racket higher.

8. _____ the cheers louder!

9. _____ all of your tomato juice.

10. _____ the basketball through the hoop!

Lesson 1.21 Imperative Sentences

Find It

Use a thesaurus to find other imperative words that
are synonyms of the imperative words below.

1. call - _____

2. carry – _____

3. drink – _____

4. drive – _____

5. look – _____

6. pass – _____

7. pick – _____

8. run – _____

9. shoot – _____

10. stop – _____

Try It

Write ten imperative sentences using the synonyms from the activity above. Remember
to use correct punctuation.

1. _____

2. _____

3. _____

4. _____

5. _____

6. _____

7. _____

8. _____

9. _____

10. _____

Lesson 1.22 Simple Sentences

Simple sentences are sentences with one independent clause. **Independent clauses** present a complete thought and can stand alone as a sentence. Simple sentences do not have any dependent clauses. **Dependent clauses** do not present a complete thought and cannot stand alone as sentences.

Simple sentences can have one or more subjects.

> The *costumes* glittered.
> The *costumes* and the *jewelry* glittered.

Simple sentences can have one or more **predicates**, or verbs.

> The *costumes* glittered.
> The costumes *glittered* and *sparkled*.

Simple sentences can have more than one subject and more than one predicate.

> The *costumes* and the *jewelry glittered* and *sparkled*.

Identify It

Underline the subject or subjects in the following simple sentences.

1. Elsa, Tanya's mom, liked baking cookies.

2. Elsa liked baking cookies and cooking spaghetti.

3. Elsa and Tanya liked baking and cooking together.

4. Elsa liked baking and cooking.

5. Elsa liked baking better.

6. Tanya liked baking and cooking.

7. Tanya liked cooking better.

8. Tanya liked eating her mom's cookies.

9. Elsa liked eating her daughter's spaghetti.

10. Tanya's friends liked coming to dinner.

Lesson 1.22 Simple Sentences

Identify It
Underline the predicate or predicates in the following simple sentences.

1. Elsa, Tanya's mom, liked baking cookies.

2. Elsa liked baking cookies and cooking spaghetti.

3. Elsa and Tanya liked baking and cooking together.

4. Elsa liked baking and cooking.

5. Elsa liked baking better.

6. Tanya liked baking and cooking.

7. Tanya liked cooking better.

8. Tanya liked eating her mom's cookies.

9. Elsa liked eating her daughter's spaghetti.

10. Tanya's friends liked eating cookies and spaghetti.

Try It
Write ten simple sentences of your own. Remember, simple sentences may have more than one subject and more than one predicate.

_____

_____

_____

_____

_____

_____

_____

_____

_____

_____

_____

Lesson 1.23 Compound Sentences

Compound sentences are sentences with two or more simple sentences (independent clauses) joined by a coordinate conjunction, punctuation, or both. As in simple sentences, there are no dependent clauses in compound sentences.

A compound sentence can be joined by a comma and a coordinate conjunction.
    The costumes glittered, *but* the jewelry was dull.

A compound sentence can also be two simple sentences joined by a semicolon.
    The costumes glittered; the jewelry was dull.

Match It
Match simple sentences in Column A with simple sentences in Column B to create compound sentences. Add either a comma with a coordinate conjunction or a semicolon.

Column A	Column B
1. The seats were bad.	The snack bar line was long.
2. The actors were funny.	We can stay late.
3. The intermission was short.	The show was good.
4. The ushers were nice.	The ticket takers were rude.
5. We can leave early.	The orchestra played well.
6. The theater lights were low.	The actors were serious.
7. The audience laughed.	The audience applauded.
8. The actors' voices were loud.	The seats were sold out.
9. The play had good reviews.	The music was soft.
10. The actors bowed.	The stage lights were bright.

Lesson 1.23 Compound Sentences

Solve It
Combine each pair of simple sentences into a compound sentence.

Simple Sentences

1. Richard likes apples. Jackie likes pears.
2. Jackie likes skating. Richard likes running.
3. Richard likes dancing. Jackie likes singing.
4. Jackie likes summer. Richard likes winter.
5. Richard likes math. Jackie likes science.

Compound Sentences

1. _____
2. _____
3. _____
4. _____
5. _____

Try It
Continue to write about what Richard and Jackie each like and don't like. Write three more sentences for each character. Then, combine the sentences to form compound sentences.

Richard

_____

_____

_____

Jackie

_____

_____

_____

Compound Sentences

_____

_____

_____

Lesson 1.24 Complex Sentences

Complex sentences have one independent clause and two or more dependent clauses. The independent and dependent clauses are connected with a subordinate conjunction or a relative pronoun. Remember, dependent clauses do not present a complete thought and cannot stand alone as sentences. The dependent clause can be anywhere in the sentence.

Common subordinate conjunctions include *after, although, as, because, before, if, since, when, where, while, until,* and *unless.*

One complex sentence (connected with subordinate conjunction):
> *Since* he got a math tutor, his math grades have improved.

The independent and dependent clauses can also be connected with relative pronouns like *who, whose, which,* and *that.*

One complex sentence (connected with relative pronoun):
> Mr. Addy, *who* is a math teacher, tutors Ashton.

Combining simple sentences into complex sentences adds variety and clarity to writing.

Identify It
Circle the letter that best answers each question.

1. Which of the following contains two simple, individual sentences?
   a. He is wearing his baseball uniform. He is holding his baseball bat.
   b. He is wearing his baseball uniform and holding his baseball bat.
   c. He is wearing his baseball uniform, although the game was cancelled.

2. Which of the following contains a compound sentence?
   a. She is eating a salad. She is drinking lemonade.
   b. She is eating a salad, and she is drinking lemonade.
   c. She is drinking lemonade, since she is thirsty.

3. Which of the following contains a complex sentence?
   a. Mary went jogging. Rose went jogging.
   b. Mary and Rose went jogging.
   c. Before they ate breakfast, Mary and Rose went jogging.

4. Which of the following contains a complex sentence?
   a. Mike was learning about moose at school. Mike was learning about caribou at school.
   b. Mike and Gil were learning about Arctic animals at school.
   c. Mike, who loved animals, was learning about moose and caribou at school.

Lesson 1.24 Complex Sentences

Rewrite It

Rewrite the following article by combining simple sentences to make compound and complex sentences.

Why would a ten-week-old piglet wander the streets of New York City? New York City animal control officers asked the same question. One Friday afternoon they found a tiny piglet. They thought she had escaped from a market. They took her to a shelter. She was treated for wounds on her legs. She was treated for a respiratory infection. The shelter staff named her Priscilla. A local sanctuary took her in. They treated her. She was quite sick. Now she is healthy. Priscilla was adopted by a family in Michigan. She loves her new home.

_____

_____

_____

_____

_____

_____

_____

_____

_____

_____

Try It

Write an article about an event in your school using compound and complex sentences. Include at least three complex and two compound sentences in your article.

_____

_____

_____

_____

_____

_____

_____

_____

Lesson 1.25 Combining Sentences

Combining short, choppy sentences into longer more detailed sentences makes writing much more interesting and much easier to read. Sentences can be combined in a variety of ways.

<u>Compound subjects and compound verbs:</u>

Brad went on a hiking trip. C.J. went on a hiking trip.
Brad and C.J. went on a hiking trip.

We hiked on our long weekend away. We biked on our long weekend away.
We hiked and biked on our long weekend away.

<u>Adjectives and adverbs:</u>

I ate an orange for breakfast. The orange was sweet.
I ate a *sweet orange* for breakfast.

Abby walked through the foggy forest. Abby walked slowly.
Abby *walked slowly* through the foggy forest.

<u>Making complex sentences (using subordinate conjunctions):</u>

The class was going on a camping trip. They were going on the trip providing it didn't rain.
The class was going on a camping trip *providing it didn't rain.*

Rewrite It

Rewrite these simple sentences into compound or complex sentences.

1. Rachel went to the carnival on Saturday. Dan went to the carnival on Saturday.

   _____

2. The popcorn crackled as it popped. The popcorn snapped as it popped.

   _____

3. Nancy investigated the old trunk. Nancy investigated the brown trunk.

   _____

4. Carson excitedly spoke about his journey. Carson loudly spoke about his journey.

   _____

5. We can stop for breakfast. We can stop for breakfast if it is quick.

   _____

Lesson 1.25 Combining Sentences

Identify It

Draw a line to match the sentences on the left with the type of combined sentences they are on the right.

1. So that the birthday party remains a surprise, we must get there on time.

   compound subjects

2. Helen and Tammy brought sweaters as presents.

   combining adjectives

3. Helen brought a purple, knit sweater.

   complex sentence

4. Ginger liked raspberry, lemon cake.

   compound verbs

5. Because it was her birthday, Ginger's mom baked her favorite cake.

   combining adjectives

6. Ginger's mother cooked and baked for hours.

   complex sentence

7. Ginger and her friends had a great time at the party.

   compound subjects

8. Ginger greatly appreciated the presents.

   combining adverbs

9. Although it was late, the friends stayed for more cake.

   complex sentence

Try It

Pretend that you are a reporter covering a birthday party. Write an account of the party. Use adjective and adverbs and both compound and complex sentences.

_____

_____

_____

_____

_____

_____

_____

_____

_____

_____

Lesson 1.26 Sentence Fragments

A **sentence fragment** is a group of words that is missing either a subject or a verb. A sentence fragment is also a group of words that doesn't express a complete thought, as in a dependent clause.

Takes a walk every day at lunch. (no subject)
Complete Sentence: *Sandy* takes a walk every day at lunch.

A walk every day at lunch. (no subject and no verb)
Complete Sentence: *Sandy takes* a walk every day at lunch.

Since the line was so long. (not a complete thought)
Complete Sentence: *We went to a different restaurant,* since the line was so long.

Match It
The sentences in Column A are sentence fragments. Choose a group of words from Column B that will complete the sentence and make it whole. Write the new sentences on the line.

Column A	Column B
1. is the twelfth month of the year.	December has two birthstones,
2. Until 46 B.C.,	December
3. Several European countries	Orville Wright made the first heavier-than-air flight at Kitty Hawk, North Carolina,
4. turquoise and zircon.	celebrate December 6th as the Feast of Saint Nicholas.
5. on December 17, 1903.	December had only 29 days.

_____

_____

_____

_____

_____

_____

_____

_____

_____

Review   Chapter I Lessons 18–27

The following paragraph is out of order. Reorder the sentences so they make sense. Rewrite the paragraph and then write what kind of paragraph it is.

It also protects our natural habitats. We should all be committed to a recycling program. The same is true with curbside pollution; less trash means less trash and pollution on our streets. Recycling greatly reduces our need for landfills. It also reduces curbside pollution. When we cut down trees, birds, squirrels, rabbits, and many other forest animals lose their homes. Recycling is important to our environment for many reasons. These are excellent reasons why we should encourage our friends and family to recycle. If we recycle the paper products we use, fewer trees will have to be cut down. Recycling saves trees. If we recycle what would be trash, there will be less garbage to put into the landfills.

_____

_____

_____

_____

_____

_____

_____

_____

_____

_____

_____

_____

_____

_____

_____

_____

_____

_____

_____

Review

Chapter 2 Mechanics

Lesson 2.1 Proper Nouns: Cities, States, Countries

The names of cities, states, and countries are considered **proper nouns** and are always capitalized.

Capitalize the names of cities:
> Anchorage   Columbus   Kona   Detroit   Los Angeles   New York

Capitalize the names of states:
> Alaska   Ohio   Hawaii   Michigan   California   New York

Capitalize the names of countries:
> United States   Mexico   Japan   Denmark   Israel

Do not capitalize the words *city*, *state*, or *country* in a sentence. These words are common nouns.

Complete It

Circle the correct answer in each of the following sentences.

1. The capital of California is (Sacramento, sacramento).

2. This (City, city) has a population of approximately 407,000.

3. (Los Angeles, los Angeles), has the largest population in California.

4. The city in the United States with the largest population is (New York, new york).

5. The (City, city) of New York has a population of approximately 22 million.

6. The capital city of the state of (New York, new york) is Albany.

7. Albany, (New York, new york) has a population of approximately 40,800.

8. The largest city in (California, california) is Los Angeles.

9. California is the most populated (State, state) in the United States.

10. The least populated state in the United States is (Wyoming, wyoming).

11. China is the most populated (Country, country).

12. The population of (China, china) is over 1.3 billion.

13. The population of the (United States, united States) is over 315 million.

14. The largest continent, Asia, is made up of 48 (Countries, countries).

15. Australia is the only continent that is its own (Country, country).

Lesson 2.1 Proper Nouns: Cities, States, Countries

Proof It
Proofread the following journal entry. Use the proofreading marks to correct capitalization errors.

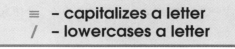

≡ – capitalizes a letter
/ – lowercases a letter

EIFFEL TOWER

Today was my fourth day in Europe. We have been traveling quickly. I feel like I'm a long way from my home in athens, Ohio. We started our trip in London, england. We saw Big Ben and the Tower of London. Then, we took the tube to paris, france. We climbed the Eiffel Tower—what an awesome view! We also saw the Mona Lisa at The Louvre Museum. France is a beautiful Country. Then, it was off to belgium. We started our tour in the City of Brugges. I have eaten many waffles in ohio, but I've never seen as many as in this Country. Tomorrow we leave belgium for munich, germany. I'm hoping to eat one of those big pretzels while I'm there. I know next year I'm taking an eating tour of Europe.

Try It
Write a journal entry about a city you have visited. Be sure to name the state, if it applies, and the country.

_____
_____
_____
_____
_____
_____
_____
_____

Lesson 2.2 — Proper Nouns: Days of the Week, Months of the Year

Days of the week and months of the year are considered **proper nouns** and are always capitalized.

Capitalize days of the week:

Sunday   Monday   Tuesday   Wednesday   Thursday   Friday   Saturday

Capitalize months of the year:

January   February   March   April   May   June
July   August   September   October   November   December

Solve It

The following sentences each contain the name of a day of the week. However, the sentences don't make sense. Unscramble the names of the days of the week so the sentences make sense. Write the day on the line after each sentence. Remember to capitalize the day of the week.

1. dswdeayen falls in the middle of the week. _____

2. The day ryifda got its name from the German word *frigga*. _____

3. The sun gave its name to nysuda. _____

4. hsruydta was named for Thor, a god in northern mythology. _____

5. On onmayd, the day of the moon, I go to school. _____

6. I play baseball on suartyad, the first day of the weekend. _____

7. Tiw's day gives its name to usedtay, honoring the northern mythological wrestler Tir. _____

January						
1	2	3	4	5	6	7
8	9	10	11	12	13	14
15	16	17	18	19	20	21
22	23	24	25	26	27	28
29	30	31				

February						
		1	2	3	4	
5	6	7	8	9	10	11
12	13	14	15	16	17	18
19	20	21	22	23	24	25
26	27	28				

March						
		1	2	3	4	
5	6	7	8	9	10	11
12	13	14	15	16	17	18
19	20	21	22	23	24	25
26	27	28	29	30	31	

April						
						1
2	3	4	5	6	7	8
9	10	11	12	13	14	15
16	17	18	19	20	21	22
23	24	25	26	27	28	29
30						

May						
	1	2	3	4	5	6
7	8	9	10	11	12	13
14	15	16	17	18	19	20
21	22	23	24	25	26	27
28	29	30	31			

June						
				1	2	3
4	5	6	7	8	9	10
11	12	13	14	15	16	17
18	19	20	21	22	23	24
25	26	27	28	29	30	

July						
						1
2	3	4	5	6	7	8
9	10	11	12	13	14	15
16	17	18	19	20	21	22
23	24	25	26	27	28	29
30	31					

August						
	1	2	3	4	5	
6	7	8	9	10	11	12
13	14	15	16	17	18	19
20	21	22	23	24	25	26
27	28	29	30	31		

September						
					1	2
3	4	5	6	7	8	9
10	11	12	13	14	15	16
17	18	19	20	21	22	23
24	25	26	27	28	29	30

October						
1	2	3	4	5	6	7
8	9	10	11	12	13	14
15	16	17	18	19	20	21
22	23	24	25	26	27	28
29	30	31				

November						
			1	2	3	4
5	6	7	8	9	10	11
12	13	14	15	16	17	18
19	20	21	22	23	24	25
26	27	28	29	30		

December						
					1	2
3	4	5	6	7	8	9
10	11	12	13	14	15	16
17	18	19	20	21	22	23
24	25	26	27	28	29	30
31						

Lesson 2.2 Proper Nouns: Days of the Week, Months of the Year

Complete It

Complete the following sentences by writing the correct month of the year on the line. Remember to capitalize the month when you write it in. Use an encyclopedia or the Internet if you need help.

1. The chrysanthemum is the flower for

   _____, the eleventh month of the year.

2. The United States celebrates Independence Day on _____ 4th.

3. _____ is the shortest month of the year.

4. In the Northern Hemisphere, summer begins in the month of _____.

5. _____ was named for the Roman emperor, Augustus.

6. Fools come out to play on this _____ day.

7. The month of _____ was named for the Roman god, Janus.

8. *Cinco de Mayo* is a holiday celebrated in Mexico on the fifth day of

   _____.

9. The sapphire is the birthstone for _____, the ninth month of the year.

10. Farmers start to bring in their crops, including pumpkins, in the month of

    _____.

11. In the Northern Hemisphere, winter begins in the month of _____.

12. It is often said that the month of _____ "Comes in like a lion and goes out like a lamb."

Try It

Write an advertisement announcing a garage sale you are going to have. Include the days of the week, dates, place, and time in your ad. Be sure to correctly capitalize all of the proper nouns.

_____

_____

_____

_____

_____

Lesson 2.3 Proper Nouns: Names of Streets, Places, People

The names of specific streets, places, and people are proper nouns and are capitalized.

Capitalize the names of specific streets.

Stanley Street   Ohio Avenue   Crosswinds Boulevard

When using the nonspecific words like *street* and *road* in a sentence, they are not capitalized.

I live one *street* over from you.

Capitalize the names of specific places.

Rocky Mountain National Park

Capitalize the first and last names of people, including special titles, initials, and abbreviations that go with the names.

President Jimmy Carter

Do not capitalize nonspecific street names, places, or titles when used without a name in a sentence.

My best friend is going to run for class president.

Identify It

Write **PN** if the sentence has a proper noun. If not, leave it blank.

1. _____ Felicia and Bryan stayed at the Lake Hotel on their vacation.

2. _____ Drive slowly on this street, many children play here.

3. _____ Dr. Edwards gave my kitty a pill that will make her feel better.

4. _____ The hotel where we stayed was beautiful.

5. _____ Cross over Breeze Loop and then turn right on Riverbend Drive.

6. _____ The president of our class will speak at the rally.

7. _____ Hawaii Volcanoes National Park is located on the island of Hawaii.

8. _____ The park has many attractions.

9. _____ The doctor was kind to her patients.

10. _____ Karl lives on Lane Road.

11. _____ The bridge connected Mill Drive to Shamrock Road.

12. _____ Dr. Green is a wonderful veterinarian.

NAME _____

Proofread the following paragraph using proofreading marks. Look for errors in the use of capitalization with proper nouns.

≡ – **capitalizes a letter**
/ – **lowercases a letter**

Do you believe in haunted houses? How about haunted hotels? Granville, Ohio, is home to the buxton inn. The buxton inn, located on broadway street, has a haunting reputation. The Hotel was built in 1812 by orrin granger, founder of the City of Granville. The Hotel was named after major buxton, who ran the inn from 1865–1905. So whose ghost has appeared in this Inn? orrin granger was first seen in the 1920s eating a piece of pie in the kitchen. major buxton has been seen by Guests, mostly in the Dining Room. The ghosts of other Owners have also been spotted. Even a kitty of days gone by has been seen roaming throughout the buxton inn. Of course the ghost cat now has a name—Major Buxton.

Try It
Write a short autobiography. Write about the city where you were born, the name of the first street where you lived, your parents' and siblings' names, and the name of your first school and first teacher. Write about a few of your favorite memories growing up. Make sure all of the proper nouns in your autobiography are capitalized.

_____

_____

_____

_____

_____

_____

_____

_____

_____

Lesson 2.4 Proper Nouns: Words Used as Names, Official Names

Words like *mother, father, aunt,* and *uncle* can be used as **proper nouns** or **common nouns**. When they are used as proper nouns, they should be capitalized.

The words *mother* and *father* can be used in place of a name. If they are, they are capitalized.

> *Mother,* where did I leave my jacket?

In the following instance, *father* is not used as a replacement of a name.

> My *father* took me to the hockey game.

The same is true for the words *aunt, uncle, grandmother,* and *grandfather.*

> *Aunt Clara* has a wonderful cat.
> My *aunt* likes to travel in the mountains.
> I like to play catch with *Uncle Richard.*
> My *uncle* was great in sports when he was in school.

Official names, such as those of businesses and their products, are capitalized. Nonspecific names of products are not capitalized, even if they follow the business or product name.

> *Papa's Pizza* (name of business)
> I like *Papa's Pizza's* pizza. (business name followed by product name)

Match It

Circle the letter that matches the description.

1. the word *mother* not used to replace a name
   a. Mother, please pass the beans.
   b. My mother was the pitcher on her softball team.

2. the word *grandfather* used as a name
   a. Grandfather Clarence was a veterinarian.
   b. My grandfather is a good cook.

3. the word *aunt* not used to replace a name
   a. My aunt has the cutest puppy.
   b. Aunt Marilyn is a teacher.

4. official business name followed by product name
   a. Oat Crisps cereal
   b. Oat Crisps

5. official business name without product name
   a. Tender Pet pet food
   b. Tender Pet

Lesson 2.4 Proper Nouns: Words Used as Names, Official Names

Solve It

Create your family tree below. Be sure to capitalize proper names. Write three different sentences about the people on this tree.

1. _____

2. _____

3. _____

Try It

What products would you like to invent? Invent some products of your own. Then, give your products an official business name. Come up with at least three business names and three product names. Be sure to capitalize the official business names.

1. _____

2. _____

3. _____

Lesson 2.5 Proper Nouns: Titles, Names of Subjects

Titles are **proper nouns** and are capitalized. The first and last words of titles are always capitalized, as well as every word in between except for articles (*a, an, the*), short prepositions (*in, of, at*), and short conjunctions (*and, but*). These words, however, should be capitalized if they are the first word in the title. Most titles are also underlined in text. Song titles and essays, however, are in quotes.

This rule applies to titles of the following: books, newspapers, magazines, articles, poems, songs, plays, movies, works of art, pictures, stories, and essays.

> book: *Catcher in the Rye*   play: *The Music Man*
> movie: *Master and Commander*   work of art: *Mona Lisa*

School subjects are capitalized if they name a specific course.
> My favorite course is *Literature and Poetry*.

Do not capitalize the names of general subjects.
> My *math* teacher is also the baseball coach.

Exception: Language subjects are all proper nouns, so they should all be capitalized.
> I am studying my *French* homework.

Complete It
Circle the correct answer that completes each of the following sentences.

1. I read (<u>The Lord of the Rings</u>, <u>the Lord Of The Rings</u>) series during summer vacation.

2. I like doing the crossword puzzle in the (<u>Chicago tribune</u>, <u>Chicago Tribune</u>).

3. My favorite song is ("Drops of Jupiter", "drops of jupiter").

4. Have you ever seen (<u>Raiders of The lost Ark</u>, <u>Raiders of the Lost Ark</u>)?

5. I have gym class after (spanish, Spanish).

6. Mr. Howard is the best (history, History) teacher.

7. Mr. Hayes teaches a course called (Geometry, geometry).

8. Can I walk with you to (Math, math) class?

9. My sister is studying (American poetry, american poetry) in college.

10. The poem ("Dawn", "dawn") by Paul Lawrence Dunbar is one of Dylan's favorites.

Lesson 2.5 Proper Nouns: Titles, Names of Subjects

Rewrite It

These reviews have errors in capitalization. Make the corrections as you rewrite them.

* Sleeper of the Year! The movie <u>Happy Times In Snoozeville</u> is for you if you need a nap. The dialogue is boring, the action is slow, and the actors can't act. Don't waste your money on this dud.

* Great Read! The <u>perfect Peach</u> is just what it says—a peach. Take this book to the beach or read it in your favorite armchair. The <u>perfect Peach</u> has rich characters and a comforting mood. Don't miss this great read.

* Ouch! My Ears! What was Kay Joe thinking when she recorded "Dancing in the desert"? She can't hit the high notes and the lyrics make no sense. The track "Singing On The Seas" is worth the money—but buy the single.

_____

_____

_____

_____

_____

_____

_____

_____

_____

Try It

Write the title of your favorites below. Don't forget to capitalize when necessary and underline or use quotes correctly.

book _____   magazine _____

movie _____   poem _____

song _____   play _____

Lesson 2.6   Sentences, Direct Quotations

The first word of every **sentence** is capitalized.
> *Build* the parfait by sprinkling the berries on the yogurt.

The first word in **direct quotations** is capitalized. Quotation marks are used to show the exact words of a speaker, a direct quotation. The quotation marks are placed before and after the exact words.
> Our teacher said, "*Please* go to the board and write your answer."
> "*I* hope I know the answer," I whispered as I walked to the board.

Indirect quotations are not capitalized. An indirect quotation does not use the exact words of a speaker and does not use quotation marks.
> The coach said he wanted to have practice three nights a week.

If a quotation is split and the second half continues, do not capitalize the second half. If a new sentence begins after the split, then capitalize it as you would with any sentence.
> "I think my puppy is the cutest in the class," said the boy, "*and* the best trained."
> "My aunt took me to the shelter to get a kitty," said Candy. "*We* found the perfect calico!"

Identify It
One of the sentences in each of the following pairs is not capitalized correctly. Write **X** on the line before the sentence that is capitalized correctly.

1. _____ The apartment was perfect for Phyllis and Marc.

   _____ the apartment was perfect for Phyllis and Marc.

2. _____ "Check out the exercise room," said Maria. "It has everything we use."

   _____ "Check out the exercise room," said Maria. "it has everything we use."

3. _____ The agent John said The pool will open in the spring.

   _____ The agent John said the pool will open in the spring.

4. _____ "Rob," said Regina, "the view is fantastic!"

   _____ "Rob," said Regina, "The view is fantastic!"

5. _____ Eddy and Jackie decided They would move next month.

   _____ Eddy and Jackie decided they would move next month.

Lesson 2.6　Sentences, Direct Quotations

Use the proofreading marks to correct the errors in capitalization.

> ☰ - capitalizes a letter
> / - lowercases a letter

"Hey, Mom," hollered Matt on his way in the house, "Guess what I learned about in school today?"

Matt knew his mother wouldn't guess. He said He would show her. he pulled a picture out of his backpack.

"Here it is, Mom," said Matt. "it's a snot otter!"

"Oh my," exclaimed his mom, "What exactly is a snot otter?"

"I knew you would ask," Matt gleefully replied. "snot otters are a type of salamander. they live in cool, fast moving streams with big rocks. They live up to 29 years. But their habitats are declining."

"That is sad," replied Matt's mother. "why are they in danger?"

"Water pollution and sediment build-up in streams are a couple of reasons they are in danger," answered Matt. "if someone finds a snot otter, it should be put back in the stream. They are not pets."

"Well, I'm glad to hear that," Matt's mom said, smiling.

Try It
Write a dialogue about a student telling a teacher about an animal. Pay attention to the capitalization of sentences in and outside of dialogue.

_____

_____

_____

_____

_____

_____

Lesson 2.7 Personal Letters

A **personal letter** has five parts: heading, salutation, body, closing, and signature. Personal letters have special punctuation.

The **heading** of a personal letter is the address of the person writing the letter and the date it is written. The name of the street, city, state, and month are all capitalized.

> 3126 Milly Dr.
> Marblehead, MI 20000
> October 5, 2006

The **salutation** is the greeting and begins with *dear*. Both *dear* and the name of the person who is receiving the letter are capitalized. Place a comma after the name.

> Dear Stanley**,**

The **body** is the main part of the letter and is capitalized just like all sentences and paragraphs.

The **closing** can be written many ways. Only the first word is capitalized. Place a comma after the closing.

> Your friend,   Sincerely,   All the best,

The **signature** is usually only your first name. It is always capitalized.

> Milton

Proof It
Proofread the personal letter. Use the proofreading marks to make corrections in capitalization.

> ≡ – capitalizes a letter
> / – lowercases a letter

5711 eastwind loop
anchorage, AK 20000
february 26, 2014

dear aunt Linda,

How have you been? I've been great. school is going very well this year. I really like social studies and english. However I've had a little trouble with math. my best friend is helping me with that.

I'm playing on the junior varsity basketball team. I love it. I think I will try out for the track team this spring.

I can't wait to see you on your next visit. Please tell uncle Ray I said hello.

With Love,
Kay

Lesson 2.7 Personal Letters

Try It

Write a personal letter. Be sure to capitalize the letter correctly. Use the information provided on page 80 if you need help setting your personal letter up correctly.

_____

_____

_____

_____

_____

_____

_____

_____

_____

_____

_____

_____

_____

_____

_____

_____

_____

_____

_____

_____

_____

_____

_____

_____

_____

_____

Review | Chapter 2 Lessons 1-7

Review: Proper Nouns: Cities, States, Countries, Days of the Week, Months of the Year, Names of Streets, Places, People, Words Used as Names, Official Names, Titles, Names of Subjects, Sentences, Direct Quotations, Personal Letters

Putting It Together

Proofread the following personal letter. Make all of the necessary capitalization corrections. Then, use the following page to rewrite the letter.

| ≡ – capitalizes a letter |
| / – lowercases a letter |

4064 palm tree lane

oakdale, FL 20000

March 19, 2014

dear Perry,

How do you like anaheim, california? Do you like your new school? things are about the same here. I'm getting ready for the baseball season. Our first game is next thursday. coach Baum says That I can start as pitcher.

The basketball team won the division, but we didn't get very far in state. I think the baseball team will do well. we already have a sponsor for the team. Fast Feet Sporting Goods has already signed on. I like Fast Feet Shoes, but I'm still going to buy my gloves from your Uncle's store.

My family is going on vacation this summer. We're going to chicago, illinois. My Grandpa and Grandma are going, too. We are going to visit aunt Christina. We're also going to the navy pier and the sears tower. Did you know that the Sears Tower used to be the tallest Building in the world?

Are you trying out for the track team this year? Aren't try-outs in march? I hope you get to come back to visit soon. maybe we can meet somewhere in the middle next winter break? Write when you can.

your Friend,

Denny

NAME

Review # Chapter 2 Lessons 1–7

Review

Lesson 2.8   Periods: After Declarative and Imperative Sentences, In Dialogue

Declarative and imperative sentences both use **periods**. A declarative sentence makes a statement. An imperative sentence demands an action be performed, and the subject is usually not expressed. Sometimes, an imperative sentence can end with an exclamation point.

> They left for their trip on Friday.
> Look at the icicle formations on the roof!

Quotation marks are used to set off direct quotations in dialogue. Quotation marks are placed before and after the direct quotation. A period is placed at the end of a direct quotation sentence when it is declarative or imperative. The period goes inside the quotation mark.

> Lori said, "I'll give the ticket to the agent."

In direct quotation sentences when the quote comes at the beginning of the sentence, use a comma at the end of the direct quotation instead of a period.

> "I'll give the ticket to the agent," said Lori.

Complete It
Add the correct punctuation mark in each sentence.

1. "My house is on the right__" said Martha.

2. Martha said__ "My house is on the right."

3. "Look at the bright plants my mom planted__"

4. "My house has plants like that__" Deidre replied.

5. Deidre continued, "We also have some bushes mixed in, too__"

Lesson 2.8 Periods: After Declarative and Imperative Sentences, In Dialogue

Proof It

Proofread the following paragraphs. Use proofreading marks to make punctuation corrections.

e	– deletes letters, words, punctuation
^	– inserts letters, words, punctuation

   "Cities, like cats, reveal themselves at night" said the British poet Rupert Brooke. Perhaps he didn't realize how true his statement is Some cats save their owners' lives when they reveal themselves at night.

   Take, for example, Aggie Aggie was a cat rescued from a shelter when she was five weeks old. Aggie was curious and playful, but not aggressive That is until one evening when she heard an intruder trying to climb through the front window Before her owners even made it downstairs, she pounced, attacked, and scared away the intruder.

   Cats also rescue and save their own. One particular cat lived in an abandoned building with her five recently born kittens When the building caught on fire what was she to do? Of course she had to save her family. One by one she carried her kittens out of the burning building to safety. She was burned and blistered but she got every one of her kittens out The firefighter who made sure the cat and kittens were safe and cared for is now known as "The Animal Guy."

Try It

Interview a friend about his or her pet. Then, write a newspaper article about it. Be sure to include direct quotations.

_____

_____

_____

_____

_____

_____

Lesson 2.9 Periods: In Abbreviations, In Initials, Titles Before Names

The **period** is used in more than just sentences. Periods are used in abbreviations, initials, and titles before names.

Use a period after each part of an abbreviation. Do not leave a space between the period and the following letter.

B.C.   A.D.   B.A.

Use a period after each letter of an initial.

Michael J. Fox   J. K. Rowling   J. R. R. Tolkien

Use a period with abbreviated titles before names.

Dr.   Mr.   Mrs.

Do not use periods if the abbreviation is an acronym. **Acronyms** are words formed from the first letters of words in a phrase.

NATO (North Atlantic Treaty Organization)

Match It

Draw a line to match the following abbreviations, titles, and acronyms in Column A with their meanings in Column B.

Column A	Column B
B.S.	Public Broadcasting System
DJ	United Nations International Children's Education Fund
PBS	District Attorney
D.A.	Disc Jockey
SCUBA	Mister
D.V.M.	Doctor of Veterinary Medicine
UNICEF	Bachelor of Science
Mr.	Self-contained underwater breathing apparatus
M.D.	Bachelor of Arts
B.A.	Medical Doctor

Lesson 2.9 Periods: In Abbreviations, In Initials, Titles Before Names

Rewrite It

The following people were either misidentified or are not pleased with how their names appeared in a recent magazine article. Rewrite them as they request.

I. Donna Kay Dell   "I prefer my middle name to be an initial."

_____

2. Melissa Sarah Oliver   "I prefer first and middle initials."

_____

3. Dr. E. Bates, Ph.D.   "I am a medical doctor."

_____

4. M. L. Roberts   "I am a doctor."

_____

5. Steven Paul Starks   "I would like my first name as an initial."

_____

Try It

You are having a formal party. Make a formal list of ten people you would like to invite. Include their titles and abbreviations, like Mr., Dr., Mrs., and M.D.

_____ _____

_____ _____

_____ _____

_____ _____

_____ _____

Lesson 2.10 Question Marks

Interrogative sentences ask questions and they are followed by **question marks**.
How many students are in the class**?**

When used in quotations, questions marks can be placed either inside or outside of the end quotation mark depending on the meaning of the sentence.

When the question mark is punctuating the quotation itself, it is placed inside the quote.
The customer asked, **"**How much does the car cost**?"**

When the question mark is punctuating the entire sentence, it is placed outside the quote.
Did the salesperson say, **"**It's the most expensive car on the lot**"?**

A question mark is unnecessary in sentences with indirect quotations.
I asked my sister if she would help us with our math homework.

Complete It
Place a question mark in the appropriate place in the sentences that need one. In the sentences that do not use a question mark, place a period at the end of the sentence.

1. Did you hear back from the admission's office

2. Jason said he saw the movie 12 times

3. My mom asked, "How much homework do you have tonight"

4. Did your teacher say, "Finish the entire chapter tonight"

5. I asked Jill if she had a good day

6. There must have been 200 people in the theatre

7. The hiker asked, "Is this as far as this trail goes"

8. The server asked if we wanted dessert

9. Are you going to play tennis with your sister this evening

10. Dr. Eric said to take the medicine once a day

11. My brother asked, "Is Judy studying with you after school"

12. Did the coach say, "Run three more laps"

Lesson 2.10 Question Marks

Proof It
Proofread the following dialogue. Make corrections using proofreading marks. Look for errors with question mark use.

> _e_ – deletes letters, words, punctuation
> ∧ – inserts letters, words, punctuation
> ⌒ – moves punctuation from one place to another

Patrick was doing a report on the Milky Way Galaxy. He asked the director of the local observatory if he could ask him some questions?

Patrick asked, "How many planets orbit the sun in our solar system"?

The director answered, "We have eight planets that orbit the sun."

Patrick asked, "Was my teacher right when she said planets are divided into two categories?"

"Yes, Patrick, Mrs. Sanchez was right," said the director. "Mercury, Venus, Earth, and Mars belong to the terrestrial planets." The director asked, "Do you know the name of the other category"?

"The other category is the Jovian planets," answered Patrick.

The director said, "You are correct!"

Patrick had a good time and learned a lot about the Milky Way Galaxy. He asked the director if he could come back again?

Try It
Choose a subject you would like to know more about. Write a dialogue between you and your teacher. Ask your teacher questions about the subject you chose. Have your teacher ask you questions in the dialogue, too.

_____

_____

_____

_____

_____

Lesson 2.11 Exclamation Points

Exclamatory sentences are sentences that express surprise and strong emotion and are punctuated with **exclamation points**.

I'm so excited you made it into the first college on your list**!**

Interjections sometimes require exclamation points.

Oh, no**!** I left my homework at home!

Identify It

Identify which sentences should have exclamation points. Place an **X** at the end of each sentence that needs an exclamation point.

1. Watch out The stove is hot _____

2. The soup should be on medium high _____

3. Thank you for my beautiful flowers _____

4. Tulips are my favorite flower _____

5. Ouch My fingers were still in the door _____

6. After all my hard work, I finally got an A on the test _____

7. I have a lot of homework to do tonight _____

8. I won the race _____

9. Oh, no The rain is coming down really hard now _____

10. I like the sound of rain on the rooftop _____

11. The cars are coming fast _____

12. My favorite color is green _____

13. The ice is slippery _____

14. Don't shut the door before getting your keys _____

15. Wait I forgot the keys _____

Lesson 2.11 Exclamation Points

Solve It

Which of the following situations would require an exclamation point? Write a short sentence for each illustration you see. Include interjections and exclamation points when you think they are necessary.

_____

_____

_____

Try It

Write six more sentences that should be written using exclamation points.

1. _____

2. _____

3. _____

4. _____

5. _____

6. _____

Lesson 2.12 Commas: Series, Direct Address, Multiple Adjectives

Commas have a variety of uses. Three uses for commas are commas in a series, commas in direct address, and commas used with multiple adjectives.

A **series** is at least three items listed in a sentence in a row. The items can be words, phrases, or clauses. Commas are used to separate them.

I must clean *the kitchen, the bathroom, and the family room* this weekend.

When the name of a person spoken to is used in a sentence, it is called **direct address**. A comma is used to separate the name of the person from the rest of the sentence.

Sarah, after our chores are done, we can go to the park.

When more than one adjective is used to describe a noun, they are separated by commas.

The *sweet, cool apple* tasted good on the hot day.

Make sure each adjective describes the noun. There is no comma in the following sentence because the pizza is not piping. The adverb *piping* describes the adjective *hot.*

The *piping hot* pizza was ready to come out of the oven

Match It

Match the following sentences in Column A to the type of commas they require in Column B. Draw a line from Column A to Column B to make the match.

Column A	Column B
1. The soft, sweet, loving kitten purred.	commas in a series
2. They stayed out of the biting cold water.	commas in direct address
3. Daphne, please answer the door.	commas separating adjectives
4. I worked out on the treadmill, bike, and elliptical cycle.	no comma necessary

Column A	Column B
5. The sizzling hot sauce was too hot to eat.	commas in a series
6. Stephanie, please pass the strawberries.	commas in direct address
7. The sweet, juicy, ripe peaches were perfect.	commas separating adjectives
8. The tennis players grabbed their towels, bags, and balls on their way off the court.	no comma necessary

Lesson 2.12 Commas: Series, Direct Address, Multiple Adjectives

Rewrite It

Rewrite the sentences, adding commas where necessary.

1. John wanted pasta vegetables and rolls for dinner.

   _____

2. Tiffany make the reservation for 7:30.

   _____

3. The new black car was just what he wanted.

   _____

4. I checked on the slowly boiling water.

   _____

5. Keith had to do his homework eat dinner and take out the trash.

   _____

Try It

Make a list of five of your favorite things. Then, make a list of words that describe these things. Write five sentences about your favorite things using the words that describe them. Be sure to include commas in the appropriate places.

1. _____   _____

   _____

2. _____   _____

   _____

3. _____   _____

   _____

4. _____   _____

   _____

5. _____   _____

   _____

Lesson 2.13 Commas: Combining Sentences, Set-Off Dialogue

Use a **comma** to combine two independent clauses with a coordinate conjunction.
    The players must be well trained, *and* they must train for at least six months.

If a sentence begins with a prepositional phrase, set it off with a comma.
    After he finishes his homework, he can talk with his friends.

Commas are also used when setting off dialogue from the rest of the sentence.
    The tour guide said, *"Today's walking tour will take us past several museums."*
    "Then, we will eat in a cafe," promised the tour guide.

Complete It
Complete the following sentences by adding commas where necessary. Not all of the sentences need commas.

1. The Teton Mountain Range is a beautiful sight and it is a challenge for rock climbers.

2. The Teton Mountain Range is located in Wyoming and the range is in part of the Grand Teton National Park.

3. Because of its beauty more than 3 million people visit each year.

4. Visitors have been known to say "This is one of the most inspiring places I've seen."

5. Millions of people gaze at the peaks yet it remains peaceful.

6. The range not only has more than 100 lakes but also 200 miles of trails.

7. Rock climbers come from all over the world to climb Grand Teton.

8. "The view from the mountain is breathtaking" said one climber.

9. While Grand Teton's highest peak is 13,700 feet other peaks attract climbers.

10. "Wildlife viewing is amazing here" said another tourist.

Lesson 2.13 Commas: Combining Sentences, Set-Off Dialogue

Proof It
Proofread the following paragraph. Add commas where necessary.

> *e* – deletes letters, words, punctuation
> ^ – inserts letters, words, punctuation

What is a marathon? Most runners know that a marathon is a foot race of 26.2 miles but not everyone knows how the marathon began. Now popular worldwide the marathon has its roots in Greece. We are familiar with bicycle couriers but ancient Greeks used foot couriers. Many of them had to run city to city to make deliveries. In 490 B.C. Persia was at war with Greece. A Persian army landed 25 miles from Athens at the city of Marathon. After a mighty battle the Greeks were victorious. A runner was sent from Marathon to Athens to spread the news of the victory. Pheidippides ran the 25 miles from Marathon to Athens. When he reached the city legend says he said "Rejoice, we conquer." Then, Pheidippides fell dead. Although the facts are not known for sure the legend prevails. The modern race got a name and the marathon was born.

Try It
Write a paragraph explaining your favorite sport, how it got its beginning, and why you like it. Use a variety of sentences. Add a quotation of your own.

_____

_____

_____

_____

_____

_____

_____

_____

Lesson 2.14 Commas: Personal Letters

The five parts of the personal letter are: **heading**, **salutation (greeting)**, **body**, **closing**, and **signature**. **Commas** appear in four of the five parts of the personal letter.

A **comma** follows the city and the date in the heading.

> 3151 Stuckey Lane
> Chicago, IL 30000
> March 7, 2008

A **comma** follows the name in the salutation.

> Dear Mary,

Follow the normal rules for using comma in sentences.

A **comma** follows the last word in the closing.

> Your friend,

^ – inserts commas

Proof It

Proof the following friendly letter. Add commas where necessary.

> 5512 Alpine Lane
>
> Ridgeview CO 55214
>
> April 26 2015
>
> Dear Marina
>
> How are you? Are you getting excited for summer? I am going to volunteer at the local animal shelter and I am going to learn all about the different kinds of animals there. I am sure that it will be a hard job but it will be rewarding, too.
>
> What are your plans for summer? Will you be going camping with your parents like you did last year? That sounds like so much fun! After you get back I want to know all about it.
>
> I need to get back to reading about animal care and I hope to hear from you soon!
>
> Your friend
>
> Sharon

NAME ______________________

Lesson 2.14 Commas: Personal Letters

Try It

Write a friendly letter of your own. Pay attention to your use of commas.

Lesson 2.15 Quotation Marks

Quotation marks are used to show the exact words of a speaker, called a **direct quotation**. The quotation marks are placed before and after the exact words.

> "I must make it to the post office before 5:00," said Sharon. "I want to get my invitations in the mail today."

Quotation marks are also used when a direct quotation is made within a direct quotation. In this case, single quotation marks are used to set off the inside quotation.

> Dylan said, "Michael, the coach said, 'Practice will be at 4:00 instead of 3:00.'"

The single quotation marks express what the coach said. The double quotation marks express what Dylan is saying as a direct quote.

Quotation marks are used with some titles. Quotation marks are used with the titles of short stories, poems, songs, and articles in magazines and newspapers.

> short story: *"A White Heron"*

If a title is quoted within a direct quotation, then single quotation marks are used.

> Hannah said, "I hope the DJ plays my favorite song, 'Purple People Eater.'"

Match It

Match the following sentences or titles from Column A to the type of quotation in Column B. Draw a line to make the match.

<u>Column A</u>	<u>Column B</u>
1. Susan said, "Let's go to lunch at 12:30."	direct quotation
2. Connie answered, "My boss said, 'Our lunch meeting is scheduled for 12:00 sharp.'"	quote within a quote
3. "Prairie Island"	title

<u>Column A</u>	<u>Column B</u>
4. "Soak Up the Sun"	direct quotation
5. My sister said, "The coach said 'Eat a good dinner thenight before the game.'"	quote within a quote
6. "I'm heading for the beach," Sheryl said.	title

Lesson 2.15 Quotation Marks

Proof It
Proofread the following dialogue using proofreading marks. Make corrections on the use of quotation marks.

> ⸜ – inserts quotations

Claude Monet lived from 1840 to 1926. He was the founder of impressionism, said Mrs. Konikow.

What is impressionism? asked Doug.

Impressionism is an art form that captures a visual image and uses colors to give the effect of reflected light. Many of Monet's paintings were landscapes, answered Mrs. Konikow.

"Did Mrs. Konikow say, Many of Monet's paintings were landscapes?" asked Patricia.

Yes, answered Doug, landscapes are stretches of scenery that can be seen in one view.

Like flower gardens? asked Patricia.

Yes, Patricia, said Mrs. Konikow, like flower gardens. Later in his life, Monet retired from Paris and moved to his home in Giverny, France, where he continued to paint. He had beautiful gardens. You can see them in books and at his house in France.

Someday, I would like to go to France, said Patricia, but for now I think I'll just take a trip to the library.

Try It
Practice writing sentences with quotation marks. Write one sentence that is a direct quotation, one that is a quote within quotes, and one that includes a title.

1. _____

2. _____

3. _____

Lesson 2.16 Apostrophes

Apostrophes are used to form contractions, possessives, and plurals.

Contractions are shortened forms of words. The words are shorted by leaving out letters. An apostrophe takes the place of the omitted letters.

I am = I'm   *let us = let's*

Possessives show possession, or ownership. To form the possessive of a singular noun, add an apostrophe and an **s**.

I have *Walt's books*.

To form the possessive of plural nouns ending in **s**, simply add the apostrophe. If the plural noun does not end in an **s**, add both the apostrophe and an **s**.

The *boys' uniforms* will be ready on Friday.
The *children's puppet show* will be performed on Wednesday.

If you are writing about more than one letter of the alphabet or number, only add **s** to form the plural.

My name has two B**s** in it.
I have two page 4**s** in my book.

Complete It

Complete the following sentences by changing words to contractions. Write the contraction on the line that follows the words.

We're	It's	He'd
I'm	We've	let's

1. (I am) _____ hungry and thirsty.

2. (We are) _____ on our way to the café.

3. (It is) _____ not too far away, and it has the best muffins.

4. Do you think we should take something back for Pablo? (He would) _____ appreciate it.

5. (We have) _____ a lot of homework to do at lunch.

6. Come on, (let us) _____ hurry.

Lesson 2.16 Apostrophes

Solve It

Look at the pictures below and write a sentence for each that identifies the object and who the object belongs to. The first one has been done for you.

1. <u>The child's toys are everywhere.</u> _____

2. _____

3. _____

4. _____

5. _____

Try It

Write how many letters are duplicated in the following names. Then, on the last line, write your name. Write how many letters are duplicated in your name. The first one has been done for you.

1. Nathan <u>2 Ns and 2 As</u> _____   5. David _____

2. Lee _____   4. McKenna _____

3. Greg _____   6. _____

Lesson 2.17 Colons

Colons are used to introduce a series, to set off a clause, for emphasis, and in time.

Colons are used to introduce a series in a sentence. Usually, but not always, the list is proceeded by the words *following, these, things*.

> The chef does the *following:* washes the vegetables, chops the vegetables, and steams the vegetables.

Colons are sometimes used instead of a comma, in more formal cases, to set off a clause.

> The weather reporter said: *"We can expect six more inches of snow overnight."*

Colons are used to set off a word or phrase for emphasis.

> We hoped to see some activity in the night sky. And then we saw it: *a shooting star.*

Colons are used when writing the time.

> Are we meeting at *9:00* or *10:00?*

Identify It

Identify why the colon is used in each sentence. Write a **S** for series, **C** for clause, **E** for emphasis, or **T** for time.

1. _____ One of the most violent storms occurs primarily in the United States: tornados.

2. _____ A tornado is defined as the following: "a violent rotating column of air extending from a thunderstorm to the ground."

3. _____ Thunderstorms that develop in warm, moist air in advance of a cold front can produce these things: hail, strong wind, and tornados.

4. _____ Tornados are most likely to occur in the spring and summer months between 3:00 pm and 9:00 pm, but can occur anytime.

5. _____ Staying aware is most important for safety. During storms, look for the following: dark, greenish skies, large hail, loud roars, and flash floods.

6. _____ You can be prepared by doing the following: developing a safety plan, practicing house drills, and listening to weather reports.

Lesson 2.17 Colons

Rewrite It

Rewrite the following passage, adding colons where needed.

> I would like to apply for the following position Latin Cultural Food Writer. I graduated from the Culinary Art Institute in New York. I have cooked dishes from many cultures Latin, French, and Middle Eastern.
>
> I have expertise in Mexican food history, culture, and cooking. When the Spanish explorer Cortez first came to America, he found many culinary surprises chocolate, peanuts, vanilla, beans, squash, avocados, coconuts, corn, and tomatoes. I have created many dishes which incorporate many of these foods and flavors.
>
> Included with this letter are the following my resume, school transcripts, and references.
>
> You can reach me weekdays between 7 00 a.m. and 3 00 p.m.

_____

_____

_____

_____

_____

_____

_____

_____

_____

_____

_____

Try It

Write four sentences, one for each type of colon use: series, clause, emphasis, and time.

1. _____

2. _____

3. _____

4. _____

Lesson 2.18 Semicolons

A **semicolon** is a cross between a period and a comma. Semicolons can be used to join two independent clauses, to separate clauses containing commas, and to separate groups which contain commas.

Semicolons join two independent clauses when a coordinate conjunction is not used.
The loud thunder scared me; I hid under my covers.

Semicolons are used to separate clauses when they already contain commas.
Although the thunder was loud, it did no harm; I emerged from my bed safe and sound.

Semicolons are also used to separate words or phrases that already contain commas.
We are looking for the following features in our new house: *a garage with space for two cars, storage, and tools; a kitchen with a refrigerator, dishwasher, stove, and microwave; and bedrooms with closets and a bathroom.*

Match It
Match the first half of the sentences in Column A with the second half in Column B. Then, circle all of the semicolons in the sentences.

Column A

1. Donna was close to home;

2. After the game was over, my team went for pizza;

3. The long shopping list included the following:

4. I didn't go to school;

5. Because we were on vacation, we weren't home to get the call;

6. Before sending the resume do the following:

Column B

I went to the doctor, instead.

it wasn't important anyway.

she had traveled a long way.

check the spelling, facts, and names; call your references; and verify the address.

we were all starving.

rye, pumpernickel, and wheat bread; lettuce, carrots, and onions for salad; and cranberry, grapefruit, and tomato juice.

Lesson 2.18 Semicolons

Proof It
Proofread the following magazine article using proofreading marks. Look for missing and out of place semicolons, and commas used instead of semicolons.

> *e* – **deletes letters, words, punctuation**
> ︿; – **inserts semicolon**

Who is Sue? Sue is a Tyrannosaurus rex she is the largest and best preserved T-rex ever discovered. Although she was discovered in South Dakota, Sue now resides in Chicago, Illinois, at The Field Museum, she is on display for the public to see. Visitors can see up close Sue's features: ribs, forelimbs, and mouth bones, CT scan of her skull the braincase as well as; many other parts. Sue is quite special she is the most complete T-rex fossil ever discovered. While we have a lot to learn about our past from Sue, we may also learn about our present and future Sue has given us much to explore.

Try It
Write four complete sentences each with two independent clauses joined by a semicolon.

_____

_____

_____

_____

_____

_____

_____

Lesson 2.19 Hyphens

Hyphens are used to divide and to create new words.

Use a hyphen to divide the word between lines. Divide words between syllables.
    sanctu-ary   *de-posit*

Do not divide a one syllable word or words with fewer than six letters.
    ball, toy, cedar, book

Divide syllables after vowels if a vowel is a syllable by itself.
    cele-brate   not: *cel-ebrate*

Do not divide one letter from the rest of the word.
    ele-phant   not: *e-lephant*

Hyphens can be used to create new words when combined with *self, ex,* or *great.*
    My *great-grandfather* worked on the railroad.

Solve It
Solve the following puzzle. Place the words from the box in the appropriate spaces. The words must be divided correctly in order to fit into the boxes.

| basket | compose | dinosaur | graduate | puppy |
| bicycle | crocodile | embankment | personal | television |

1. __ __ __ __ - __ __ __ __ __ __ __

2. __ __ __ - __ __ __

3. __ __ __ - __ __ __ __ __

4. __ __ __ __ __ - __ __ __ __

5. __ __ __ __ __ - __ __ __

6. __ __ __ - __ __ __ __

7. __ __ __ __ __ __ - __ __ __ __

8. __ __ __ __ - __ __ __

9. __ __ __ __ __

10. __ __ __ __ - __ __ __ __

Lesson 2.19 Hyphens

Proof It

The words in this advertisement are broken in the wrong places. Use the proofreading marks to correct the placement of the hyphens.

ℓ	– **deletes letters, words, punctuation**
∧	– **inserts letters, words, punctuation**
↶	– **moves punctuation from one place to another**

Come and see what's wild in Alaska. Anchorage, A-laska, in South central Alaska, is home to a wide variety of wildlife. Anchorage is one of the best cities in the world to view nat-ure and wildlife at its best. All year long, you are able to see wildlife: moose, caribou, bears, dall sheep, wolves, whales, ly-nx, and otters. At the Alaska Wildlife Conservation Center, you can see wildlife in a special environment. The Alaska Wildlife Conserv-ation Center is a non-profit organization that serves as a refuge for orphaned, injured, and ill animals. The center also educates vis-itors about Alaskan wildlife. The Tony Knowles Trail; a biking, hiking, and ski trail that runs through Anchorage, is also an excellent viewing spot for wildlife. Just be careful, we are invading their homes. Treat all an-imals you see with respect, and with distance. Come and take a walk on our wild side. Visit Anchorage, Alaska!

Try It

How many *self's, ex's,* and *great's* can you think of? Write at least two of each that start with these prefixes and a hyphen. Use a dictionary if you need help.

1. _____
2. _____
3. _____
4. _____
5. _____
6. _____

7. _____
8. _____
9. _____
10. _____
11. _____
12. _____

Lesson 2.20 Parentheses

Parentheses are used to show extra material, to set off phrases in a stronger way than commas, and to enclose numbers.

Supplementary, or extra, **material** is a word or phrase that gives additional information.
> Those apples *(the ones in the basket)* are good for baking in cobblers.

Sometimes, words or phrases that might be set off with commas are set off with parentheses, instead. It gives the information more emphasis for a stronger phrase.
> The television program, *the one that was canceled*, was my favorite.
> The television program *(the one that was canceled)* was my favorite.

Parentheses are also used to enclose numbers in a series.
> I do not want to go to the movie because *(1)* it is too late, *(2)* it is all the way across town, and *(3)* it is too scary.

Complete It

Complete the following sentences by adding parenthetical phrases from the box to the sentences. Add the parentheses where they belong. The first one is done for you.

(1) (2) (3) with four doors	(1) (2) (3) my best friend	my great-great-grandmother's see key

1. The road on this map looks like a two-lane road.

   The road on this map (see key) looks like a two-lane road.

2. The recipe is the best!

   _____

3. Andy is moving to another state.

   _____

4. I love to exercise because it is good for my heart, it gives me energy, and I feel good afterward.

   _____

   _____

5. The new, blue car is the one I want.

   _____

6. Pigs are my favorite animal because they are intelligent, cute, and make "oinking" sounds.

   _____

Lesson 2.20 Parentheses

Rewrite It

Rewrite the following paragraph. Add parentheses as needed.

The Japanese Tea Ceremony is an ancient and beautiful ritual. The ceremony is 1 a way of preparing tea, 2 a way of serving tea, and 3 a way of drinking tea. The room where the tea ceremony is held is the teahouse called *chashitsu*. One particular tea ceremony, *Chaji*, is held to honor guests into a home. The guests 1 enter the tea house from the garden called *roji*, 2 are served a light meal, 3 take a short break in the garden, 4 return to the tea house. At this time, the host 1 prepares a thick tea called koicha, and 2 prepares a thin tea. Lafcadio Hearn an author of books about Japan and Japanese fairy tales said, "The tea ceremony requires years of training and practice... yet the whole of this art, as to its detail, signifies no more than the making and serving of a cup of tea."

_____

_____

_____

_____

_____

_____

_____

_____

_____

_____

_____

_____

Try It

Write one sentence that has supplemental material in parentheses, one sentence that sets off information with emphasis, and one sentence that has numbers and parentheses.

1. _____

2. _____

3. _____

Review Chapter 2 Lessons 8–20

Review: Periods: After Declarative and Imperative Sentences, In Dialogue, In Abbreviations, In Initials, Titles Before Names, Question Marks, Exclamation Points

Putting It Together

The following sentences are missing punctuation. Add periods, question marks, and exclamation points where needed.

1. Don't forget to stop by the store and pick up bread on your way home from school

2. What time is Gillian stopping over

3. Helen said, "The flowers in my garden are beautiful"

4. Look out

5. J R R Tolkien is my favorite author.

6. My dentist is Dr Guten.

7. Do I have an appointment with Dr. Guten on Tuesday

8. Ellen Hobbs, MA is speaking at our school on Friday.

Review: Commas: Series, Direct Address, Multiple Adjectives, Combining Sentences, Set-Off Dialogue, Personal Letters

Proofread the following letter. Add commas where necessary using proofreading marks.

⌃ – inserts commas

6919 Muirfield Rd.
Bloomfield MI 30000
September 23 2015

Dear Vijay

    I wanted to write you and tell you about my weekend. I went to the Ryder Cup and I saw my favorite players! The Ryder Cup is a golf match between the United States and Europe. It is the only team golf match with a real history. I got to see Tiger Woods Sergio Garcia and Jay Haas. Although you can't say anything during the course of play I yelled out "Tiger you're the best!" between holes. It was great. I bought you a hat at the gift shop and I'll give it to you when I see you winter break. I hope you are well.

Your friend
Mindy

Review Chapter 2 Lessons 8–20

Review: Quotation Marks, Apostrophes, Colons, Semicolons, Hyphens, Parentheses

Rewrite each sentence. Add punctuation where necessary.

1. My great grandmother played softball in college, said Aidan.

   _____

   _____

2. The doctor said "You'll be fine!"

   _____

   _____

3. I want to take Ms. Roses class because 1 she teaches a lot of geography, 2 she takes her classes on field trips, and 3 she is nice.

   _____

   _____

4. "Charlotte, did our teacher say, the bus for the museum leaves at 9 00?"

   _____

   _____

5. I am excited about going to the museum of art I want to be an artist someday.

   _____

   _____

6. Susan got what she had been hoping for a new job.

   _____

   _____

7. I didnt read the series, <u>The Lord of the Rings</u>, but I loved the movies.

   _____

   _____

Chapter 3 Usage

Lesson 3.1   Irregular Verbs

The **present tense** of a verb tells that the action is taking place now or continuously.
> I *do* the crossword puzzles on Sunday.

The **past tense** of a verb tells that the action took place in the past.
> Renee and Kristen *went* on an archeological dig last semester.

The **past participle** of a verb tells that the action began in the past and was completed in the past. In order to form the past participle, the verb must be preceded by one of the following verbs: *was, were, has, had,* or *have.*
> Yuki, Lori, and Blair *had come* with us on our vacation three years in a row.

Complete It

Complete the following sentences by circling the correct verb in parentheses.

1. Timmy (come, has come) over for dinner every night this week.

2. I can (did, do) my homework now.

3. The class (go, had gone) to the same exhibit last year.

4. Please (came, come) and pick up your order.

5. Andrea (do, has done) that assignment many times before.

6. The butterflies (had come, has come) back to this same location for many years.

7. Bianca and Nicole (gone, went) to see the butterflies at the butterfly house.

8. Meg (did, was done) with her chores before the programs started.

9. Ollie (came, come) home from his vacation with many pictures.

10. Trinity and Eddie (go, gone) to the same vet as Eric and Shane.

Lesson 3.1   Irregular Verbs

Proof It
Proofread the following paragraph. Use the proofreading marks to correct errors with the use of the verbs *run, see,* and *sit*. Use clues from the rest of the sentence as to what the tense of the sentence should be.

> *e* – **deletes letters, words, punctuation**
> ^ – **inserts letters, words, punctuation**

They have ran, follow, sniff, have seen, and sometimes they sat. They are an important member of many teams. Who are they? They are rescue dogs. Rescue dogs are important to police departments, fire departments, and many rescue organizations. Rescue dogs can saw and smell things human beings can't. Human rescuers saw these dogs had run through wildernesses looking for missing persons, sniffing for clues along the way. Some dogs ran up snowy mountains to find fallen hikers and skiers. Sometimes they have sat for hours waiting for their turn to seek and rescue. And when they are called, they are ready to go.

Rescue dogs and their guardians are well trained teams. They work together, ran together, play together, and rescue together. These teams go through many hours of intensive training and see and experienced many types of challenging situations. We owe a lot to these hard-working dogs and those who train and love them.

Many believe that rescue dogs run with their noses to the ground in order to pick up scents. It's not necessarily true; rescue dogs can be trained to receive scents from the air and can ran with noses up!

Try It
Practice writing the present, past, and past participle forms of the verbs *run, see,* and *sit*. Write one sentence of each type for each verb.

_____

_____

_____

Lesson 3.2 Comparative and Superlative Adjectives

Adjectives modify, or describe, nouns. **Comparative adjectives** compare two nouns, and **superlative adjectives** compare three or more nouns.

cute/cuter/cutest   *big/bigger/biggest*   *light/lighter/lightest*

<u>Describing one noun:</u> Phoebe has a *cute* puppy.

<u>Comparing two nouns:</u> Joe's sandwich is *bigger* than Barney's.

<u>Comparing three or more nouns:</u> My windbreaker is the *lightest* jacket in my closet.

The word *more* before an adjective means it is **comparative**, comparing two nouns. The word *most* before an adjective means it is **superlative**, comparing three or more nouns. The words *more* and *most* are usually used instead of **er** and **est** with adjectives that have more than two syllables.

> Students in the morning class are *more energetic* than students in the afternoon class.
> Please sign the three yellow forms first; they are *most important*.

Complete It
Complete the following sentences by circling the correct word or words in parentheses.

1. Of the three bats, Henry's is the (light, lightest).

2. Christina has a very (cute, cuter) kitten.

3. My notebook is (bigger, biggest) than yours.

4. (Light, Lightest) rain fell on the roof.

5. Every mother thinks her child is the (cute, cutest) in the class.

6. After playing soccer, Aaron has a (big, bigger) appetite.

7. I think the cartoon at 8:30 is (cuter, cutest) than the cartoon at 8:00.

8. Jordan's bookbag is (lighter, lightest) than Riley's.

9. Gillian wants to ride on the (big, bigger) roller coaster in the park.

10. Aubrey drew her parents a (cute, cuter) picture.

11. Adam has a (bigger, biggest) lead in the race than Lewis.

12. Of all the boxes, Joe picked the (lighter, lightest) to carry.

Lesson 3.2 Comparative and Superlative Adjectives

Identify It

Identify each of the following sentences as either a comparative sentence or a superlative sentence. Write **C** for comparative and **S** for superlative. Then, underline the adjectives (including the words *more* or *most*) in the sentences.

1. _____ The most challenging sports competition in the world is the Tour de France.

2. _____ The Tour de France can be ridden in some of the worst weather conditions.

3. _____ One of the best shirts to earn in the Tour de France is the polka-dot jersey.

4. _____ The world's most famous bicyclers come to France to compete.

5. _____ Athletes now have more specialized training than they did years ago.

6. _____ The more training an athlete has, the more prepared they will be.

Try It

Write a paragraph describing a performance or sporting event you have seen. Use at least six comparative or superlative adjectives.

_____

_____

_____

_____

_____

_____

_____

_____

_____

_____

Lesson 3.3 Adjectives and Adverbs

Adverbs modify verbs, adjectives, and other adverbs. Some adverbs are easily confused with adjectives.

Bad is an adjective and *badly* is an adverb. Determine what you are modifying before using *bad* and *badly*.

> A *bad* storm is heading our way.

Bad is used as an adjective modifying the noun *storm*. No **ly** is added.

> Cami sings *badly*.

Badly is used as an adverb modifying the verb *sings*. Use the **ly** form of *bad*.

Good is an adjective and *well* is an adverb. Determine what you are modifying before using *good* and *well*.

Claudia is a *good* cook and bakes *well*, too.

In this sentence, the adverb *well* modifies the verb *bakes*. The adjective *good* modifies the noun *cook*.

The words *very* and *really* are both adverbs.

> Please talk *very* softly in the library.

The adverb *very* modifies the adverb *softly* that modifies the verb *talk*.

Complete It
Complete the following sentences by circling the correct word in parentheses. Underline the word that it modifies. Then, write what type of word it modifies: **V** for verb, **ADJ** for adjective, **ADV** for adverb, and **N** for noun.

1. _____ Jim was sick, so he ran (bad, badly) during the race.

2. _____ Amy had a great day and ran (good, well) in her race.

3. _____ The day I lost the race was a (bad, badly) day for me.

4. _____ I was a (bad, badly) beaten runner.

5. _____ But it was a (good, well) day for my friend.

6. _____ She accepted her praises (good, well).

7. _____ I will train harder so I do (good, well) in my next race.

8. _____ That will be a (good, well) day for the whole team.

Lesson 3.4 Negatives and Double Negatives

Rewrite It

As you rewrite the paragraph, correct the double negatives.

Firefighting is a brave and courageous job. If you can't imagine yourself not working hard, then this job isn't for you. Firefighters go through special training. They don't never take training lightly. Some trainees don't make it through this training. Firefighters must train in actual fires. They may find they don't like climbing no ladders that are so high. Some may find they aren't scarcely strong enough. The firefighters who graduate are ready for the job. They don't know nothing about what lies ahead, but they are trained and ready. Firefighters keep us, our pets, and our homes safe. Firefighting is a brave and courageous career to explore.

_____

_____

_____

_____

_____

_____

_____

_____

_____

_____

_____

_____

_____

Try It

Write four negative sentences using each of the following words: *not, nobody, nowhere,* and *nothing.* Do not use double negatives.

_____

_____

_____

_____

Lesson 3.5 Synonyms and Antonyms

Synonyms are words that have the same, or almost the same, meaning. Using synonyms can help you avoid repeating words and can make your writing more interesting.

    clever, smart   reply, answer   wreck, destroy   applaud, clap

Antonyms are words that have opposite meanings.

    wide, narrow   accept, decline   break, repair   borrow, lend

Identify It

Read each sentence below. If the underlined words are synonyms, write **S** on the line. If they are antonyms, write **A** on the line.

1. _____ Do you know if the house at the end of the street is <u>vacant</u> or <u>occupied</u>?

2. _____ Although Tamika is <u>shy</u> now, I don't expect that she'll be <u>timid</u> her whole life.

3. _____ The hero of the story was <u>courageous</u>, and he was rewarded for being so <u>brave</u>.

4. _____ The plane <u>departs</u> at 11:00 and <u>arrives</u> at its destination at 2:30.

5. _____ The <u>commander</u> was well respected by his men, and they were happy to follow their <u>leader</u>.

6. _____ After visiting the <u>ancient</u> ruins, it seemed odd to return to our <u>modern</u> hotel.

7. _____ I'd like you to predict whether the water will <u>expand</u> or <u>contract</u> as it freezes.

8. _____ It has been <u>gusty</u> all morning, but I'm hoping it won't be so <u>windy</u> this afternoon.

9. _____ The <u>weary</u> traveler was too <u>exhausted</u> to continue along the trail.

10. _____ If you <u>fail</u> at something once, it doesn't mean you'll never <u>succeed</u>.

Lesson 3.7   Multiple-Meaning Words

Read each sentence. On the line, write the definition
for the **boldface** word.

1. Selma left her shoes on the **bank** of the river.

   _____

   I need to stop at the **bank** and make a deposit.

   _____

2. Did you **change** the way you wear your hair? _____

   The cashier handed Kendall her **change**. _____

3. The race was **close**, but Henry won. _____

   Close the door when you come inside. _____

4. The Crestview Cougars show great team **spirit**. _____

   Have you heard the rumor that a **spirit** haunts the old McAllister mansion? _____

   _____

5. **Sign** your name on the line. _____

   Jose put up a **sign** in the hallway that advertised the school bake sale. _____

   _____

Try It
Write two sentences for each multiple-meaning word below. If you need help, you may
use a dictionary, either in book form or online.

1. wind _____

   _____

2. rock _____

   _____

3. content _____

   _____

4. fine _____

   _____

5. light _____

   _____

6. wave _____

   _____

Lesson 3.8   Similes and Metaphors

A **simile** is a figure of speech that compares two things using the words *like* or *as*.

> Ansel slept *as soundly as a bear* in winter.
> The firecrackers boomed *like thunder* across the sky.

A **metaphor** is a figure of speech that compares two unlike things that are similar in some way.

> *The grass* was *a cool carpet* beneath Marisa's feet.
> *Aunt Hattie* was *a mama bear* when it came to protecting her children.

Similes and metaphors make writing more interesting and vivid for the reader.

Identify It

Read each sentence below. On the line, write **S** if it contains a simile and **M** if it contains a metaphor.

1. _____ The full moon was a plump, friendly face peeking over the hill.

2. _____ In the middle of rush hour, the highway was a parking lot.

3. _____ Chase was excited to go, but his brother moved as slowly as molasses.

4. _____ The hail felt like tiny stinging bees as it pelted my skin.

5. _____ Rico is a night owl--he rarely goes to bed before midnight.

6. _____ The wildflowers by the side of the road were as colorful as a bag of confetti thrown into the air.

7. _____ The skater was a graceful swan as she glided across the ice.

8. _____ In the sunlight, the creek sparkled like stars in the night sky.

9. _____ The dinosaur's teeth shone like rows of small white daggers.

10. _____ Jazmin is a walking dictionary—she has an amazing vocabulary.

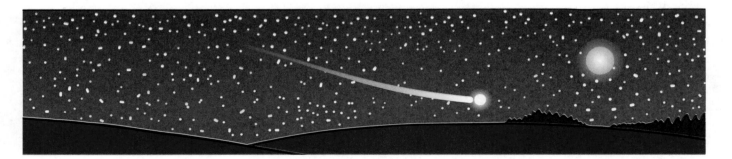

Lesson 3.8 Similes and Metaphors

Complete It
Read each item below. On the line, write a simile or metaphor to describe it.

1. the freshly fallen snow

   _____

   _____

2. the crowd in the stadium

   _____

3. the sand on the beach

   _____

4. the nervous girl

   _____

5. the fuzzy puppy

   _____

6. the sweet ice cream

   _____

7. the icy ski slope

   _____

8. the empty playground

   _____

Try It
On the lines below, describe an experience you've had or a trip you've taken. Use at least two similes and two metaphors.

_____

_____

_____

_____

_____

_____

Lesson 3.9 Idioms and Proverbs

An **idiom** is an expression that doesn't actually mean what it says. For example, "to beat around the bush" means "to avoid something."

a heart of gold = to be very kind   a drop in the bucket = a small amount

A **proverb** is a saying, an observation, or a piece of advice. The proverb "A watched pot never boils" means that when you are waiting or watching for something to happen, it takes a long time.

A picture is worth a thousand words. = A picture communicates much more to a viewer than words do.

Complete It

Use the words in the box to complete each proverb below.

| grow | crying | cloud | cat | well |
| eye | saved | eggs | boils | heart |

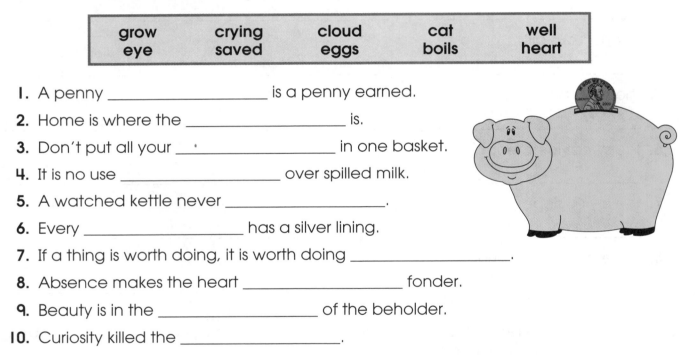

1. A penny _____ is a penny earned.

2. Home is where the _____ is.

3. Don't put all your _____ in one basket.

4. It is no use _____ over spilled milk.

5. A watched kettle never _____.

6. Every _____ has a silver lining.

7. If a thing is worth doing, it is worth doing _____.

8. Absence makes the heart _____ fonder.

9. Beauty is in the _____ of the beholder.

10. Curiosity killed the _____.

Review Chapter 3 Lessons 1–9

Review: Comparative and Superlative Adjectives

Identify the correct use of adjectives and adverbs by circling the correct answer in parentheses.

1. Stephanie thought "The Wizard of Oz" was the (cute, cutest) play she had seen all year.

2. We have to climb over one (big, biggest) rock in order to pass the test.

3. That is the (bigger, biggest) mountain I've ever seen.

4. Clint makes (more, most) money mowing lawns than Perry does selling lemonade.

5. The ice storm we had last night was (worse, worst) than the one we had last year.

6. The blizzard brought the (more, most) snow I had ever seen.

7. I think swimming in the lake in the winter is a (bad, badly) idea.

Review: Synonyms, Antonyms, and Multiple-Meaning Words

In each sentence below, a pair of words is underlined. On the line, write **S** if the words are synonyms, **A** if they are antonyms, or **M** if they are multiple-meaning words.

1. _____ Do you store your summer clothes in the <u>attic</u> or the <u>basement</u>?

2. _____ Be careful that when you <u>bow</u>, your <u>bow</u> doesn't slip out of your hair.

3. _____ The <u>presents</u> are on the table, and the guests can't wait for you to open your <u>gifts</u>.

4. _____ Did Rascal <u>eat</u> the entire bone, or did he <u>consume</u> only part of it?

5. _____ That bread is <u>stale</u>, but I did make some <u>fresh</u> bread today.

6. _____ Mom put Clare's <u>down</u> comforter <u>down</u> the laundry chute.

Chapter 4

Lesson 4.1   Writer's Guide: Prewriting

The five steps of the writing process are **prewriting**, **drafting**, **revising**, **proofreading**, and **publishing**.

Prewriting, the first stage of the writing process, involves planning and organizing. This is the stage where you get the ideas for your paper and start plotting it out.

When you prewrite, you:

- Think of ideas for your topic that are not too narrow or too broad. Write down your chosen ideas.

- Select your favorite topic, the one you think you can write about the best.

- Write down anything that comes to your mind about your chosen topic. Don't worry about grammar and spelling at this stage. This is called *freewriting*.

- Organize your information the way you might organize it in your paper. Use a graphic organizer. Graphic organizers visually represent the layout and ideas for a written paper. Graphic organizers include spider maps, Venn diagrams, story boards, network trees, and outlines.

- Use your graphic organizer to find out what information you already know and what information you need to learn more about.

Prewriting Example

Assignment: biography of a hero

Topic ideas: Martin Luther King, Jr., Eleanor Roosevelt, Jesse Owens, Cleveland Amory, Lance Armstrong, Rachel Carson

Freewriting of selected topic: Cleveland Amory hero of animals. Author. Founder of the Fund for Animals. Wrote The Cat Who Came for Christmas Read Black Beauty as a child and wanted a ranch for rescued animals. Established Black Beauty Ranch for rescued animals.

Graphic organizer:

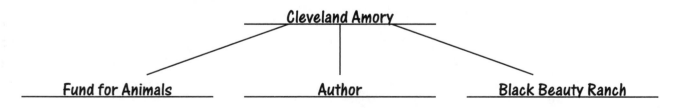

Lesson 4.2 Writer's Guide: Drafting

Drafting involves writing your rough draft. Don't worry too much about grammar and spelling. Write down all of your thoughts about the subject, based on the structure of your graphic organizer.

When you draft, you:

- Write an **introduction** with a topic sentence. Get your readers' attention by stating a startling statistic or asking a question. Explain the purpose of your writing.

- Write the **body** of your paper. Use your graphic organizer to decide how many paragraphs will be included in your paper. Write one paragraph for each idea.

- Write your **conclusion**. Your conclusion will summarize your paper.

Drafting Example

My hero was a hero: a hero to animals. Cleveland Amory (1917-1998) was an author, an animal advocate, and an animal rescuer. Reading Black Beauty as a child inspired a dream for Amory. Cleveland Amory made his dream a reality.

Amory founded The Fund for Animals. The Fund for Animals is an animal advocacy group that campaigns for animal protection. Amory served as its president, without pay, until his death in 1998. Cleveland Amory was an editor. He was an editor for The Saturday Evening Post. He served in World War II. After world war II, he wrote history books that studied society. He was a commentator on The Today Show, a critic for TV guide, a columnist for Saturday Review. Amory especially loved his own cat, Polar Bear, who inspired him to write three instant best-selling books: The Cat Who Came for Christmas, The Cat and the Curmudgeon, and The Best Cat Ever.

When Amory read Black Beauty as a child. When he read Black Beauty, he dreamed of place where animals could roam free and live in caring conditions. The dream is real at Black Beauty Ranch, a sanctuary for abused and abandoned animals The ranch's 1,620 acres serve as home for hundreds of animals, including elephants, horses, burros, ostriches, chimpanzees, and many more. Black Beauty Ranch takes in unwanted, abused, neglected, abandoned, and rescued domestic and exotic animals.

Cleveland Amory is my hero because he is a hero. He worked to make his dreams realities. His best-selling books, the founding of The Fund for Animals, and the opening of Black Beauty Ranch are the legacy of his dreams. Words from Anna Sewell's Black Beauty, the words that inspired Cleveland Amory, are engraved at the entrance to Black Beauty Ranch: "I have nothing to fear; and here my story ends. My troubles are all over, and I am at home." Cleveland Amory died on October 15, 1998. He is buried at Black Beauty Ranch, next to his beloved cat, Polar Bear.

Lesson 4.3 Writer's Guide: Revising

Revising is the time to stop and think about what you have already written. It is time to rewrite.

When you revise, you:

- Add or change words.
- Delete unnecessary words or phrases.
- Move text around.
- Improve the overall flow of your paper.

Revising Example (body of paper)

Cleveland Amory did more than just write about the animals he loved.

in 1967   one of the world's most active

Amory founded The Fund for Animals. The Fund for Animals is an animal advocacy

rights and

group that campaigns for animal protection. Amory served as its president, without

Amory extended his devotion to animals with Black Beauty Ranch

started his writing career as

pay, until his death in 1998. Cleveland Amory was an editor. He was an editor for The

serving in

Saturday Evening Post. He served in World War II. After world war II he wrote history

books that studied society. He was a commentator on The Today Show, a critic for

Amory's love of animals, as well as great affection for

TV guide, a columnist for Saturday Review. Amory especially loved his own cat, Polar

led

Bear, who inspired him to write three instant best-selling books: The Cat Who Came for

Christmas, The Cat and the Curmudgeon, and The Best Cat Ever.

Cleveland Amory made his childhood dream come true in 1979 when he
opened Black Beauty Ranch in Texas.

H

When Amory read Black Beauty as a child. When he read Black Beauty, he

dreamed of place where animals could roam free and live in caring conditions. The

for hundreds of ◄

dream is real at Black Beauty Ranch, a sanctuary for abused and abandoned animals

The ranch's 1,620 acres serve as home for hundreds of animals, including elephants,

animals

horses, burros, ostriches, chimpanzees, and many more. Black Beauty Ranch takes in

unwanted, abused, neglected, abandoned, and rescued domestic and exotic animals.

Lesson 4.4 Writer's Guide: Proofreading

Proofreading is the time to look for more technical errors.

When you proofread, you:

- Check spelling.
- Check grammar.
- Check punctuation.

Proofreading Example (body of paper after revision)

Cleveland Amory started his writing career as an editor for The <u>Saturday Evening Post</u>. After serving in <u>w</u>orld <u>w</u>ar II, he wrote history books that studied society. He was a commentator on <u>The Today Show</u>, a critic for <u>TV gⁱⁱⁱⁱⁱⁱⁱⁱⁱⁱ TV guide</u>, and a columnist for <u>Saturday Review</u>. Amory's love of animals, as well as great affection for his own cat, Polar Bear, led him to three instant best-selling books: <u>The Cat Who Came for Christmas</u>, <u>The Cat and the Curmudgeon</u>, and <u>The Best Cat Ever</u>.

Cleveland Amory did more than just write about the animals he loved. Amory founded The Fund for Animals in 1967. The Fund for Animals is one of the world's most active animal advocacy group that campaigns for animal rights and protection. Amory served as its president, without pay, until his death in 1998. Amory extended his devotion to animals with Black Beauty Ranch.

Cleveland Amory made his childhood dream come true in 1979 when he opened Black Beauty Ranch in Texas. He dreamed of place where animals could roam free and live in caring conditions. The dream is real for hundreds of unwanted, abused, neglected, abandoned, and rescued domestic and exotic animals at Black Beauty Ranch. The ranch's 1,620 acres serve as home for elephants, horses, burros, ostriches, chimpanzees, and many more animals.

Lesson 4.5   Writer's Guide: Publishing

Publishing is the fifth and final stage of the writing process. Write your final copy and decide how you want to publish your work. Here is a list of some ideas:

- Read your paper to family and classmates.

- Illustrate and hang class papers in a "Hall of Fame" in your class or school.

- Publish your work in a school or community newspaper or magazine.

Publishing (compare to the other three versions to see how it has improved)

Biography of a Hero: Cleveland Amory

My hero was a hero: a hero to animals. Cleveland Amory (1917-1998) was an author, an animal advocate, and an animal rescuer. Reading <u>Black Beauty</u> as a child inspired a dream for Amory. Cleveland Amory made his dream a reality.

Cleveland Amory started his writing career as an editor for <u>The Saturday Evening Post</u>. After serving in World War II, Amory wrote history books that studied society. He was a commentator on <u>The Today Show</u>, a critic for <u>TV Guide</u>, and a columnist for <u>Saturday Review</u>. Amory's love of animals, as well as great affection for his own cat Polar Bear, led him to three instant best-selling books: <u>The Cat Who Came for Christmas</u>, <u>The Cat and the Curmudgeon</u>, and <u>The Best Cat Ever</u>.

Cleveland Amory did more than just write about the animals he loved. Amory founded The Fund for Animals in 1967. The Fund for Animals is one of the world's most active animal advocacy groups that campaigns for animal rights and protection. Amory served as its president, without pay, until his death in 1998. Amory extended his devotion to animals with Black Beauty Ranch.

Cleveland Amory made his childhood dream come true in 1979 when he opened Black Beauty Ranch in Texas. He dreamed of a place where animals could roam free and live in caring conditions. The dream is real for hundreds of unwanted, abused, neglected, abandoned, and rescued domestic and exotic animals at Black Beauty Ranch. The ranch's 1,620 acres serve as home for elephants, horses, burros, ostriches, chimpanzees, and many more animals.

Cleveland Amory is my hero because he is a hero. He worked to make his dreams realities. His best-selling books, the founding of The Fund for Animals, and the opening of Black Beauty Ranch are the legacy of his dreams. Words from Anna Sewell's <u>Black Beauty</u>, the words that inspired Cleveland Amory, are engraved at the entrance to Black Beauty Ranch: "I have nothing to fear; and here my story ends. My troubles are all over, and I am at home." Cleveland Amory died on October 15, 1998. He is buried at Black Beauty Ranch, next to his beloved cat, Polar Bear.

Lesson 4.6 Writer's Guide: Evaluating Writing

When you are evaluating your own writing and the writing of others, being a critic is a good thing.

You can learn a lot about how you write by reading and rereading papers you have written. As you continue to write, your techniques will improve. You can look at previous papers and evaluate them. How would you change them to improve them knowing what you know now?

You can also look at the writing of others: classmates, school reporters, newspaper and magazine writers, and authors. Evaluate their writing, too. You can learn about different styles from reading a variety of written works. Be critical with their writing. How would you improve it?

Take the points covered in the Writer's Guide and make a checklist. You can use this checklist to evaluate your writing and others' writing, too. Add other items to the checklist as you come across them or think of them.

Evaluation Checklist

❑ Write an introduction with a topic sentence that will get your readers' attention. Explain the purpose of your writing.

❑ Write the body with one paragraph for each idea.

❑ Write a conclusion that summarizes the paper, stating the main points.

❑ Add or change words.

❑ Delete unnecessary words or phrases.

❑ Move text around.

❑ Improve the overall flow of your paper.

❑ Check spelling.

❑ Check grammar.

❑ Check punctuation.

❑ _____

❑ _____

❑ _____

Lesson 4.7 Writer's Guide: Writing Process Practice

The following pages may be used to practice the writing process.

Prewriting

Assignment: _____

_____

Topic ideas: _____

_____

_____

Freewriting of selected topic: _____

_____

_____

_____

_____

_____

_____

_____

_____

_____

_____

_____

Graphic Organizer:

Lesson 4.7 Writer's Guide: Writing Process Practice

Drafting

_____

_____

_____

_____

_____

_____

_____

_____

_____

_____

_____

_____

_____

_____

_____

_____

_____

_____

_____

_____

_____

_____

_____

_____

_____

_____

_____

_____

Lesson 4.7 Writer's Guide: Writing Process Practice

Revising

_____
_____
_____
_____
_____
_____
_____
_____
_____
_____
_____
_____
_____
_____
_____
_____
_____
_____
_____
_____
_____
_____
_____
_____
_____
_____
_____
_____

NAME ______________________

Lesson 4.7 Writer's Guide: Writing Process Practice

Proofreading

Lesson 4.7 Writer's Guide: Writing Process Practice

Publishing

Final Draft

_____
_____
_____
_____
_____
_____
_____
_____
_____
_____
_____
_____
_____
_____
_____
_____
_____
_____
_____
_____
_____
_____
_____
_____
_____
_____
_____
_____
_____

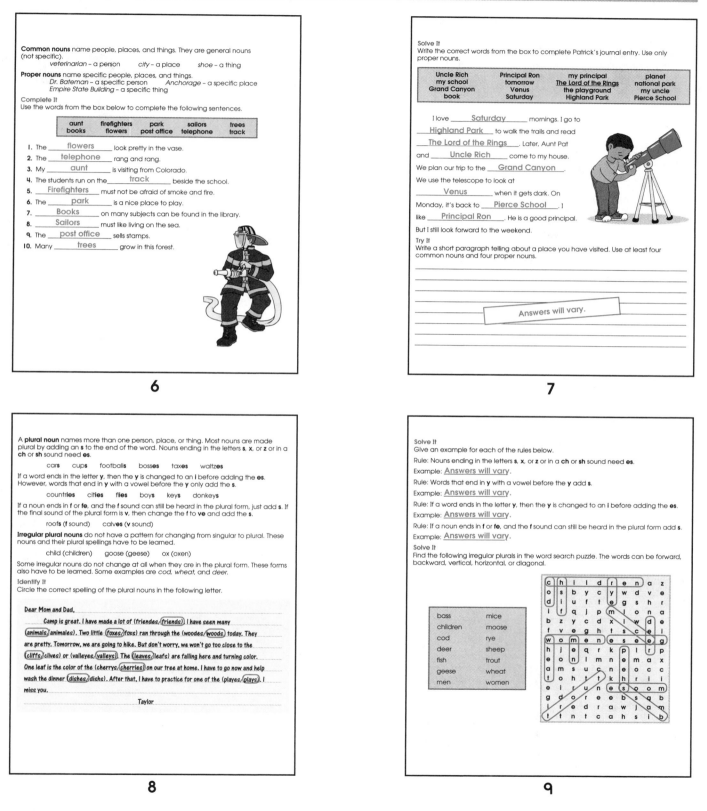

Common nouns name people, places, and things. They are general nouns (not specific).

veterinarian – a person   city – a place   shoe – a thing

Proper nouns name specific people, places, and things.

Dr. Bateman – a specific person   Anchorage – a specific place
Empire State Building – a specific thing

Complete It
Use the words from the box below to complete the following sentences.

| aunt | firefighters | park | sailors | trees |
| books | flowers | post office | telephone | track |

1. The ___flowers___ look pretty in the vase.
2. The ___telephone___ rang and rang.
3. My ___aunt___ is visiting from Colorado.
4. The students run on the___track___ beside the school.
5. ___Firefighters___ must not be afraid of smoke and fire.
6. The ___park___ is a nice place to play.
7. ___Books___ on many subjects can be found in the library.
8. ___Sailors___ must like living on the sea.
9. The ___post office___ sells stamps.
10. Many ___trees___ grow in this forest.

6

Solve It
Write the correct words from the box to complete Patrick's journal entry. Use only proper nouns.

Uncle Rich	Principal Ron	my principal	planet
my school	tomorrow	The Lord of the Rings	national park
Grand Canyon	Venus	the playground	my uncle
book	Saturday	Highland Park	Pierce School

I love ___Saturday___ mornings. I go to ___Highland Park___ to walk the trails and read ___The Lord of the Rings___. Later, Aunt Pat and ___Uncle Rich___ come to my house. We plan our trip to the ___Grand Canyon___. We use the telescope to look at ___Venus___ when it gets dark. On Monday, it's back to ___Pierce School___. I like ___Principal Ron___. He is a good principal. But I still look forward to the weekend.

Try It
Write a short paragraph telling about a place you have visited. Use at least four common nouns and four proper nouns.

Answers will vary.

7

A **plural noun** names more than one person, place, or thing. Most nouns are made plural by adding an **s** to the end of the word. Nouns ending in the letters **s**, **x**, or **z** or in a **ch** or **sh** sound need **es**.

cars   cups   footballs   bosses   taxes   waltzes

If a word ends in the letter **y**, then the **y** is changed to an **i** before adding the **es**. However, words that end in **y** with a vowel before the **y** only add the **s**.

countries   cities   flies   boys   keys   donkeys

If a noun ends in **f** or **fe**, and the **f** sound can still be heard in the plural form, just add **s**. If the final sound of the plural form is **v**, then change the **f** to **ve** and add the **s**.

roofs (f sound)   calves (v sound)

Irregular plural nouns do not have a pattern for changing from singular to plural. These nouns and their plural spellings have to be learned.

child (children)   goose (geese)   ox (oxen)

Some irregular nouns do not change at all when they are in the plural form. These forms also have to be learned. Some examples are cod, wheat, and deer.

Identify It
Circle the correct spelling of the plural nouns in the following letter.

Dear Mom and Dad,

Camp is great. I have made a lot of (friendes/(friends)) I have seen many (animals)/animales). Two little (foxes)/foxs) ran through the (woodes/(woods)) today. They are pretty. Tomorrow, we are going to hike. But don't worry, we won't go too close to the (cliffs)/clives) or (valleyes/(valleys)). The (leaves)/leafs) are falling here and turning color. One leaf is the color of the (cherrys/(cherries)) on our tree at home. I have to go now and help wash the dinner (dishes)/dishs). After that, I have to practice for one of the (playes/(plays)). I miss you.

Taylor

8

Solve It
Give an example for each of the rules below.

Rule: Nouns ending in the letters **s**, **x**, or **z** or in a **ch** or **sh** sound need **es**.
Example: ___Answers will vary___.

Rule: Words that end in **y** with a vowel before the **y** add **s**.
Example: ___Answers will vary___.

Rule: If a word ends in the letter **y**, then the **y** is changed to an **i** before adding the **es**.
Example: ___Answers will vary___.

Rule: If a noun ends in **f** or **fe**, and the **f** sound can still be heard in the plural form add **s**.
Example: ___Answers will vary___.

Solve It
Find the following irregular plurals in the word search puzzle. The words can be forward, backward, vertical, horizontal, or diagonal.

bass	mice
children	moose
cod	rye
deer	sheep
fish	trout
geese	wheat
men	women

9

Spectrum Language Arts
Grade 5

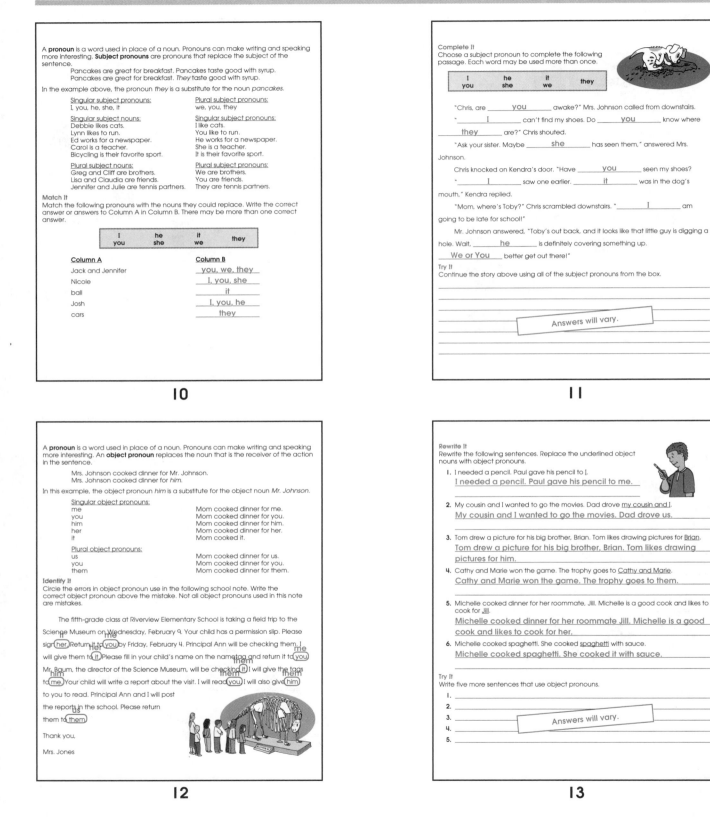

A **pronoun** is a word used in place of a noun. Pronouns can make writing and speaking more interesting. **Subject pronouns** are pronouns that replace the subject of the sentence.

Pancakes are great for breakfast. Pancakes taste good with syrup.
Pancakes are great for breakfast. *They* taste good with syrup.

In the example above, the pronoun *they* is a substitute for the noun *pancakes*.

Singular subject pronouns:
I, you, he, she, it

Plural subject pronouns:
we, you, they

Singular subject nouns:
Debbie likes cats.
Lynn likes to run.
Ed works for a newspaper.
Carol is a teacher.
Bicycling is their favorite sport.

Singular subject pronouns:
I like cats.
You like to run.
He works for a newspaper.
She is a teacher.
It is their favorite sport.

Plural subject nouns:
Greg and Cliff are brothers.
Lisa and Claudia are friends.
Jennifer and Julie are tennis partners.

Plural subject pronouns:
We are brothers.
You are friends.
They are tennis partners.

Match It
Match the following pronouns with the nouns they could replace. Write the correct answer or answers to Column A in Column B. There may be more than one correct answer.

| I | he | it | | they |
| you | | she | we | |

Column A	Column B
Jack and Jennifer	you, we, they
Nicole	I, you, she
ball	it
Josh	I, you, he
cars	they

10

Complete It
Choose a subject pronoun to complete the following passage. Each word may be used more than once.

| I | he | it | | they |
| you | she | we | |

"Chris, are _____ you _____ awake?" Mrs. Johnson called from downstairs.

"_____ I _____ can't find my shoes. Do _____ you _____ know where _____ they _____ are?" Chris shouted.

"Ask your sister. Maybe _____ she _____ has seen them," answered Mrs. Johnson.

Chris knocked on Kendra's door. "Have _____ you _____ seen my shoes?

"_____ I _____ saw one earlier. _____ it _____ was in the dog's mouth," Kendra replied.

"Mom, where's Toby?" Chris scrambled downstairs. "_____ I _____ am going to be late for school!"

Mr. Johnson answered, "Toby's out back, and it looks like that little guy is digging a hole. Wait, _____ he _____ is definitely covering something up. _____ We or You _____ better get out there!"

Try It
Continue the story above using all of the subject pronouns from the box.

_____

_____

_____

Answers will vary.

_____

_____

_____

11

A **pronoun** is a word used in place of a noun. Pronouns can make writing and speaking more interesting. An **object pronoun** replaces the noun that is the receiver of the action in the sentence.

Mrs. Johnson cooked dinner for Mr. Johnson.
Mrs. Johnson cooked dinner for *him*.

In this example, the object pronoun *him* is a substitute for the object noun *Mr. Johnson*.

Singular object pronouns:
me
you
him
her
it

Mom cooked dinner for me.
Mom cooked dinner for you.
Mom cooked dinner for him.
Mom cooked dinner for her.
Mom cooked it.

Plural object pronouns:
us
you
them

Mom cooked dinner for us.
Mom cooked dinner for you.
Mom cooked dinner for them.

Identify It
Circle the errors in object pronoun use in the following school note. Write the correct object pronoun above the mistake. Not all object pronouns used in this note are mistakes.

The fifth-grade class at Riverview Elementary School is taking a field trip to the Science Museum on Wednesday, February 9. Your child has a permission slip. Please sign (her). Return it to (you) by Friday, February 4. Principal Ann will be checking them. I will give them to (it). Please fill in your child's name on the nametag and return it to (you). Mr. Baum, the director of the Science Museum, will be checking (it). I will give the tags to (me). Your child will write a report about the visit. I will read (you). I will also give (him) to you to read. Principal Ann and I will post the reports in the school. Please return them to (them).

Thank you,

Mrs. Jones

12

Rewrite It
Rewrite the following sentences. Replace the underlined object nouns with object pronouns.

1. I needed a pencil. Paul gave his pencil to I.
   I needed a pencil. Paul gave his pencil to me.

2. My cousin and I wanted to go the movies. Dad drove my cousin and I.
   My cousin and I wanted to go the movies. Dad drove us.

3. Tom drew a picture for his big brother, Brian. Tom likes drawing pictures for Brian.
   Tom drew a picture for his big brother, Brian. Tom likes drawing pictures for him.

4. Cathy and Marie won the game. The trophy goes to Cathy and Marie.
   Cathy and Marie won the game. The trophy goes to them.

5. Michelle cooked dinner for her roommate, Jill. Michelle is a good cook and likes to cook for Jill.
   Michelle cooked dinner for her roommate Jill. Michelle is a good cook and likes to cook for her.

6. Michelle cooked spaghetti. She cooked spaghetti with sauce.
   Michelle cooked spaghetti. She cooked it with sauce.

Try It
Write five more sentences that use object pronouns.

1. _____
2. _____
3. _____   Answers will vary.
4. _____
5. _____

13

A **pronoun** replaces a noun in a sentence. The noun that is replaced is called the **antecedent**. All pronouns have antecedents. Pronouns must agree in gender and number with their antecedents and what their antecedents refer to.

Tony must bring his own lunch to the picnic.
He must bring *his* own lunch to the picnic. (agrees in gender)
Not: *He* must bring *her* own lunch to the picnic. (does not agree in gender)

Tony must bring *three* lunches to the picnic.
Tony must bring *them* to the picnic. (agrees in number)
Not: Tony must bring *it* to the picnic. (does not agree in number)

Complete It
Circle the correct pronoun in parentheses. Remember that pronouns must agree in both gender and number.

1. Austin did well on (her, (his)) English report.
2. Austin didn't do well on ((his), its) math test.
3. He missed eight problems. (He, (They)) were hard.
4. Charlotte did well on ((her), his) math test.
5. Charlotte didn't do well on ((her), them) English report.
6. She made six mistakes in grammar. ((They), She) were spelling and punctuation errors.
7. Austin tutored Charlotte with (its, (her)) grammar skills.
8. Charlotte tutored Austin with ((his), her) math skills.
9. Charlotte took Austin to dinner at ((her), them) father's restaurant.
10. They ate a small veggie pizza. (Its, (It)) was delicious.
11. Charlotte and Austin also went to see a movie. (She, (They)) went to see a comedy.
12. The movie was funny, and ((it), they) made them both laugh.

14

Solve It
Solve the following riddle by choosing words from the box to fill in the blanks.

his	it
her	them

Who ate the pizza with pepper?
Who ate the pizza with _____ it _____?
Charlotte ate the pizza with pepper.
She ate _____ her _____ pizza with _____ it _____.
Who ordered a salad with tomatoes?
Who ordered a salad with _____ them _____?
Austin ordered the salad with tomatoes.
He ordered _____ his _____ salad with _____ them _____.
I like pizza with **Answers will vary.** (fill in your favorite)
I like pizza with **Answers will vary.** (word from the box)
I like salad with **Answers will vary.** (fill in your favorite)
I like salad with **Answers will vary.** (word from the box)

Try It
Write a letter to your best friend telling about a recent event at school. Include at least four pronouns and antecedents in your letter.

_____
_____
_____
_____

| Answers will vary. |

_____
_____
_____

15

A **verb** is a word that tells the action or the state of being in a sentence. Add **ed** to the present tense of a regular verb to make it past tense. If the word already ends in the letter **e**, just add the letter **d**.

The dogs *sniff* the flowers. (present)   The dogs *sniffed* the flowers. (past)

Irregular verbs do not follow the same rules as regular verbs when forming their past tense. They must be learned. Below is a list of some of the common irregular verbs in their present and past tense forms.

Present:
am begin bring do eat get is let put rise sleep think

Past:
was began brought did ate got was let put rose slept thought

Complete It
Use a present- or past-tense verb to complete each sentence below. There is more than one correct answer.

1. Quinten _____ asked _____ a good question in science class earlier.
2. As they look at the picture, the ladies _____ gasp _____ at its beauty.
3. I _____ look _____ at the stars as I walk through the planetarium.
4. Kelly and Taylor, please _____ note _____ that in your report.
5. Shelly and Dylan _____ call _____ when they are late.
6. The spectators _____ yelled _____ and cheered many times during the game last night.
7. Jim fell on the ice. But he _____ joked _____ about it later.
8. _____ Warn _____ the passengers, now!
9. May I have some milk? I want to _____ add _____ it to my coffee.
10. Carl _____ ordered _____ waffles for breakfast.

16

Proof It
Proofread the following paragraph. Use the proofreading marks to delete the irregular present and past tense verbs that are used incorrectly. Write the correct word above the incorrect word. Use a dictionary if you need help.

| _e_ – deletes words or letters |
| ^ – inserts words or letters |

know
Do you ~~knew~~ the name of the very first national
is   a
park? It ~~was~~ Yellowstone National Park. ~~It~~ founded in
sits
1872. Yellowstone ~~sat~~ in three states: Wyoming,
Montana, and Idaho. Hot springs cut into the land of
Yellowstone. Old Faithful and Mammoth Hot Springs
get
~~got~~ the most attention from visitors. The spray from Old
rise
Faithful can ~~rose~~ 150 feet into the air. Mammoth Hot
grow
Springs continues to ~~grew~~ to this day. Many animals
live
~~lived~~ in the park. Bears, mountain sheep, elk, bison, moose, and deer, and other wildlife
make   come
~~made~~ their home in Yellowstone National Park. Thousands of visitors ~~came~~ to the park
every year.

Try It
Choose four present and four past tense irregular verbs from the list on page 16. Write a fictional paragraph using these verbs.

_____
_____
_____

| Answers will vary. |

_____
_____

17

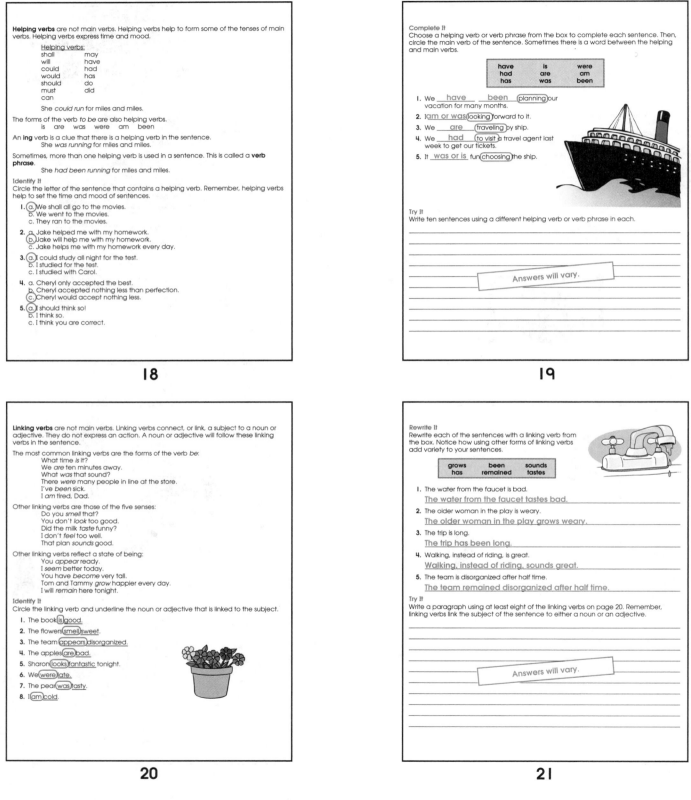

Helping verbs are not main verbs. Helping verbs help to form some of the tenses of main verbs. Helping verbs express time and mood.

Helping verbs:
shall   may
will   have
could   had
would   has
should   do
must   did
can

She *could run* for miles and miles.

The forms of the verb *to be* are also helping verbs.
is   are   was   were   am   been

An **ing** verb is a clue that there is a helping verb in the sentence.
She *was running* for miles and miles.

Sometimes, more than one helping verb is used in a sentence. This is called a **verb phrase**.
She *had been running* for miles and miles.

Identify It
Circle the letter of the sentence that contains a helping verb. Remember, helping verbs help to set the time and mood of sentences.

1. a. We shall all go to the movies.
   b. We went to the movies.
   c. They ran to the movies.

2. a. Jake helped me with my homework.
   b. Jake will help me with my homework.
   c. Jake helps me with my homework every day.

3. a. I could study all night for the test.
   b. I studied for the test.
   c. I studied with Carol.

4. a. Cheryl only accepted the best.
   b. Cheryl accepted nothing less than perfection.
   c. Cheryl would accept nothing less.

5. a. I should think so!
   b. I think so.
   c. I think you are correct.

18

Complete It
Choose a helping verb or verb phrase from the box to complete each sentence. Then, circle the main verb of the sentence. Sometimes there is a word between the helping and main verbs.

have   is   were
had   are   am
has   was   been

1. We ___have___ been (planning) our vacation for many months.
2. I am or was (looking) forward to it.
3. We ___are___ (traveling) by ship.
4. We ___had___ (to visit) a travel agent last week to get our tickets.
5. It ___was or is___ fun (choosing) the ship.

Try It
Write ten sentences using a different helping verb or verb phrase in each.

Answers will vary.

19

Linking verbs are not main verbs. Linking verbs connect, or link, a subject to a noun or adjective. They do not express an action. A noun or adjective will follow these linking verbs in the sentence.

The most common linking verbs are the forms of the verb *be*:
What time *is* it?
We *are* ten minutes away.
What *was* that sound?
There *were* many people in line at the store.
I've *been* sick.
I *am* tired, Dad.

Other linking verbs are those of the five senses:
Do you *smell* that?
You don't *look* too good.
Did the milk *taste* funny?
I don't *feel* too well.
That plan *sounds* good.

Other linking verbs reflect a state of being:
You *appear* ready.
I *seem* better today.
You have *become* very tall.
Tom and Tammy *grow* happier every day.
I will *remain* here tonight.

Identify It
Circle the linking verb and underline the noun or adjective that is linked to the subject.

1. The book (is) good.
2. The flowers (smell) sweet.
3. The team (appears) disorganized.
4. The apples (are) bad.
5. Sharon (looks) fantastic tonight.
6. We (were) late.
7. The pear (was) tasty.
8. I (am) cold.

20

Rewrite It
Rewrite each of the sentences with a linking verb from the box. Notice how using other forms of linking verbs add variety to your sentences.

grows   been   sounds
has   remained tastes

1. The water from the faucet is bad.
   The water from the faucet tastes bad.
2. The older woman in the play is weary.
   The older woman in the play grows weary.
3. The trip is long.
   The trip has been long.
4. Walking, instead of riding, is great.
   Walking, instead of riding, sounds great.
5. The team is disorganized after half time.
   The team remained disorganized after half time.

Try It
Write a paragraph using at least eight of the linking verbs on page 20. Remember, linking verbs link the subject of the sentence to either a noun or an adjective.

Answers will vary.

21

Verb tenses tell when in time something happened. The **present perfect** shows that something happened in the past and is still going on.
The Wilkinsons *have been picking* berries here for over a decade.

The **past perfect** shows that an action was completed before another action in the past.
Yoko *had thought* about taking a photography class years before she registered.

The **future perfect** shows that an action will be completed before a before future time or a future action.
By the end of the summer, we *will have visited* the pool more than 50 times!

Identify It
Underline the perfect tense in each sentence below.

1. I <u>have watched</u> backyard birds for many years.
2. I <u>had noticed</u> that my yard was very quiet during the winter.
3. The birds <u>had gone</u> elsewhere to find food.
4. I <u>have been excited</u> to see who comes to visit me now.
5. I <u>have been adding</u> new feeders to my yard every year.
6. By next winter, I <u>will have built</u> three more wooden feeders.
7. I also <u>will have stocked</u> each one with a different kind of bird seed.
8. These tiny visitors <u>have added</u> a touch of color to my days.

22

Rewrite It
Read each sentence. On the line, write the **boldface** verb in the past, present, or future perfect tense. The words in parentheses will tell you which tense to use.

1. Audrey **volunteer** at Lakeside Waterfowl Rescue. (present perfect)
   has been volunteering
2. Aisha **work** with Audrey for the last six months. (present perfect)
   has been working
3. They **rescue** dozens of ducks, geese, herons, and other birds every month. (past perfect)
   had rescued
4. The rescue **provide** fresh food and water every day, rain or shine. (past perfect)
   had provided
5. They **raise** lots of money every year. (past perfect)
   had raised
6. The rescue **rely** on its volunteers to take care of the animals since its doors first opened. (present perfect)
   has been relying
7. At the end of the summer, Audrey **earn** an award for hours donated. (future perfect)
   will have earned
8. By next fall, Aisha **receive** the same award. (future perfect)
   will have received

Try It
Write three sentences of your own about a place you have volunteered or might like to volunteer. Write one in the past perfect, one in the present perfect, and one in the future perfect.

Answers will vary, but one sentence should be in the past perfect, one in the present perfect, and one in the future perfect.

23

Verb tense shifts happen when a writer changes from one tense to another in the same sentence. Being consistent with the time frame of a piece of writing is important. It helps the reader follow what is happening.

The gardener *rolled* up his sleeves and *starts* working.

The verb *rolled* is in the past tense, and *starts* is in the present tense. The sentence should be edited to say, "The gardener *rolls* up his sleeves and *starts* working." or "The gardener *rolled* up his sleeves and *started* working."

Complete It
Complete each sentence below with the word in parentheses. Make sure that the verb tense you choose is consistent with the rest of the sentence.

1. My family pulled up to the cabin and ___unloaded___ the car. (unload)
2. We ___stay___ at the same cabin every year, and I love it. (stay)
3. In the 1960s, Grandpa Leo ___chopped___ all the logs by hand and built it himself. (chop)
4. The inside is not fancy but it ___is___ homey and cozy. (is)
5. Mom filled the fridge with groceries, and Dad ___started___ a fire in the fireplace. (start)
6. Since the fireplace is huge, it ___warms___ the small cabin quickly. (warm)
7. When I was six, I ___burned___ my hand roasting marshmallows in the fireplace. (burn)
8. Next year, we will come in June, and we ___will meet___ my cousins here. (meet)

24

Proof It
Read the selection below. There are seven places where the verb tense shifts. Use proofreading marks to correct the errors. Write the correct tense of each incorrect verb above it.

> ℰ – deletes words or letters
> ^ – inserts words or letters

Have you ever heard of the artist Andy Goldsworthy? He is probably not what you picture when you ~~thought~~ *think* of an artist. Andy ~~doesn't~~ use a canvas and paints, and he ~~didn't~~ sculpt metal or clay. Andy ~~was~~ *is* an artist who uses the elements of nature to create art. For example, he connects and arranges colorful leaves in a brook and then ~~photographed~~ *photographs* them. He made a star out of icicles or an arch out of sea pebbles and then ~~photographs~~ *photographed* it. Sometimes, creating art can be frustrating. Andy has carefully arranged scenes and ~~watches~~ *watched* the wind knock down his work. The weather has ruined pieces and ~~changes~~ *changed* his plans many times. However, none of this slows Andy Goldsworthy down. He loves his work and his interactions with nature—snow, feathers, pebbles, flowers, and branches.

Try It
Write a short paragraph. Include several verb tense shifts. Trade papers with a friend and see if you can find and correct each other's errors.

Answers will vary but should include shifts in verb tense.

25

Answer Key

Verbs must agree in number with the subject of the sentence. If the subject is singular, use a singular verb. If the subject is plural, make sure to use a plural verb.

> The shirt *fits* just right.   The movies *were* sold out.

If the subject is a **compound subject**, two or more subjects, connected by the word *and*, then a plural verb is needed.

> Erika and Chris *photograph* the birds.   Erika *photographs* the birds.

If the subject is a compound subject connected by the words *or* or *nor*, then the verb will agree with the subject that is closer to the verb.

> Neither Wanita nor Susan *likes* chocolate pie. (Susan likes)
> Do Wanita or her sisters *like* chocolate pie? (sisters like)

If the subject and the verb are separated by a word or words, be sure that the verb still agrees with the subject.

> Susan, as well as her coworkers, *wants* to complete the project. (Susan wants)

If the subject is a **collective noun**, a singular word that represents a group, like *family* and *team*, then a singular verb is generally used.

> The family *is* ready to go.   The team *runs* one mile every day.

When using the phrases *there is*, *there are*, *here is*, and *here are*, make sure that the subjects and verbs agree.

> There is one piece of pizza left.   Here is the right path to take.
> There are many pieces left.   Here are the bikes we're supposed to use.

Complete It
Circle the correct verb for each sentence.

1. Troy (help, (helps)) his sister with her homework after school.
2. Troy and Billy ((help), helps) their sister with her homework after school.
3. Does Sally or her brothers ((bike), bikes) to school?
4. There ((is), are) one store that I like at that mall.
5. Here (is, (are)) the books on that subject.

26

Proof It
Proofread the following paragraph, correcting the subject-verb agreement mistakes as you go. Use the proofreading key to mark the mistakes and insert the correction.

> ⌐ – deletes words or letters
> ∧ – inserts words or letters

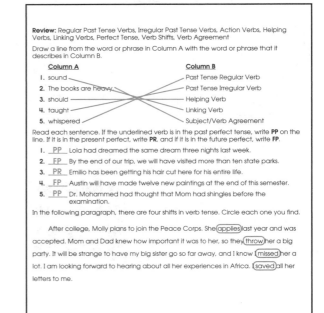

Tiger Woods' real first name is Eldrick, and he ~~were~~ was born on December 30, 1975. Fans all over the world salute**s** him as one of the greatest golfers of all time. He became a professional golfer in 1996. In 2001, Tiger held all four professional major championships at one time, the first golfer ever to do so. He ~~were~~ was also the first golfer of African American or Asian descent to win a major championship. No sportsperson ~~have~~ has ever been awarded <u>Sports Illustrated</u> Sportsman of the Year twice—except Tiger. Tiger and his father started the Tiger Woods Foundation. The foundation support**s** community-based programs that promote health, education, and welfare for children. So, how did Tiger get**s** his nickname? Tiger ~~were~~ was named after a Vietnamese soldier who was a friend of his father. Tiger's father had given the same nickname to his friend.

Try It
Write a paragraph with four sentences about your favorite sport. Be sure that the subjects and verbs agree.

_____

_____

Answers will vary.

_____

_____

27

Review: Common Nouns, Proper Nouns, Regular Plurals, Irregular Plurals, Subject Pronouns, Object Pronouns, Pronoun Agreement

Putting It Together
Answer the following questions by circling the letter of the best answer.

1. Which sentence contains a common noun?
   a. I visited Yellowstone National Park.
   (b.) I liked seeing the animals.
   c. I heard that you went to Everglades National Park.

2. Which sentence contains a proper noun?
   (a.) The U.S. Capitol is in Washington, D.C.
   b. History is one of my favorite subjects.
   c. I like to study science.

3. Which sentence contains a regular plural noun?
   a. I liked seeing the moose at the park.
   b. The geese were in the pond and then they flew overhead.
   (c.) The cats liked playing together.

4. Which sentence contains an irregular plural noun?
   a. The dogs loved playing in the water.
   b. Rabbits make great pets.
   (c.) The mice scurried under the floorboards.

5. Which sentence contains a subject pronoun?
   a. Ava went on a science field trip.
   (b.) She went on a science field trip.
   c. Aaron went on a science field trip.

6. Which sentence contains an object pronoun?
   (a.) The team captain picked me.
   b. The team captain picked Sandy to play.
   c. He picked the best player to be on his side.

7. Which sentence has an incorrect use of pronoun agreement?
   (a.) The brothers left his jackets on the field.
   b. Diane picked up her books at the library.
   c. Jason forgot his books at the library.

28

Review: Regular Past Tense Verbs, Irregular Past Tense Verbs, Action Verbs, Helping Verbs, Linking Verbs, Perfect Tense, Verb Shifts, Verb Agreement

Draw a line from the word or phrase in Column A with the word or phrase that it describes in Column B.

Column A	Column B
1. sound	Past Tense Regular Verb
2. The books are heavy.	Past Tense Irregular Verb
3. should	Helping Verb
4. taught	Linking Verb
5. whispered	Subject/Verb Agreement

Read each sentence. If the underlined verb is in the past perfect tense, write **PP** on the line. If it is in the present perfect, write **PR**, and if it is in the future perfect, write **FP**.

1. _PP_ Lola had dreamed the same dream three nights last week.
2. _FP_ By the end of our trip, we will have visited more than ten state parks.
3. _PR_ Emilio has been getting his hair cut here for his entire life.
4. _FP_ Austin will have made twelve new paintings at the end of this semester.
5. _PP_ Dr. Mohammed had thought that Mom had shingles before the examination.

In the following paragraph, there are four shifts in verb tense. Circle each one you find.

After college, Molly plans to join the Peace Corps. She (applies) last year and was accepted. Mom and Dad knew how important it was to her, so they (throw) her a big party. It will be strange to have my big sister go so far away, and I know (missed) her a lot. I am looking forward to hearing about all her experiences in Africa. I (saved) all her letters to me.

29

Adjectives are words used to describe a noun or pronoun. Using colorful, lively, descriptive adjectives makes writing and speaking more interesting.

Most adjectives are **common adjectives** and are not capitalized. They can be found before or after the noun they describe.

      It was a *breezy* day.   The day was *breezy*.

The adjective *breezy* tells something about, or describes, the noun *day*.

Proper adjectives are formed from proper nouns and are always capitalized.

      The chef likes baking his pizzas in the *Italian* oven.

The proper adjective *Italian* describes what kind of oven it is.

Solve It
Unscramble the words to reveal adjectives that might describe a butterfly.

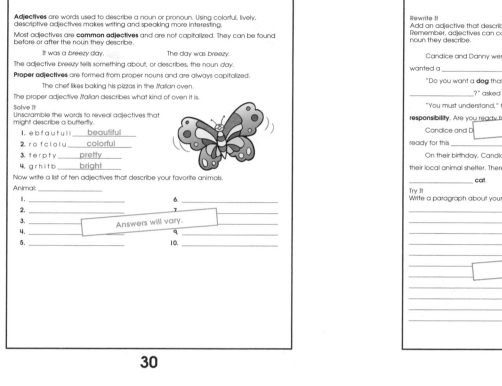

1. e b f a u t u l i   __beautiful__
2. r o f c l o l u   __colorful__
3. t e r p t y   __pretty__
4. g r h i t b   __bright__

Now write a list of ten adjectives that describe your favorite animals.

Animal: _____

1. _____   6. _____
2. _____   7. _____
3. _____   Answers will vary.
4. _____   9. _____
5. _____   10. _____

30

Rewrite It
Add an adjective that describes each noun in bold. Remember, adjectives can come before or after the noun they describe.

Candice and Danny were 12-year-old twins. They wanted a _____ **pet** for their birthday.

"Do you want a **dog** that is _____ or a **cat** that is _____?" asked their mother.

"You must understand," their mother continued, "pets are a _____ **responsibility**. Are you ready for this _____

Candice and D_____ ~~Answers will vary.~~ _____ always kind to animals, and they were ready for this _____ **job**.

On their birthday, Candice and Danny's _____ **parents** took them to their local animal shelter. There, they found a **dog** that was _____ and a _____ **cat**.

Try It
Write a paragraph about your favorite movie using ten different adjectives.

_____
_____
_____
_____
_____
Answers will vary.
_____
_____
_____
_____

31

Adverbs are words used to describe a verb, an adjective, or another adverb. An adverb tells *how, why, when, where, how often,* and *how much.* Adverbs often end in **ly** (but not always).

    How?   **Where?**
John drove *carefully* on the slick road. The weather *outside* was rainy. It seemed

    How often?   **When?**   **How?**
like it would *never* stop raining. *Tomorrow, hopefully* the weather will be better.

Identify It
Circle the letter of the sentence that contains an adverb. Remember, adverbs modify verbs, adjectives, and other adverbs.

1. (a.) Lisa quickly finished work so she could go to dinner.
   b. Lisa finished work so she could go to dinner.
   c. Lisa did not finish her work.

2. a. Rachel cooked as if for a feast.
   b. Rachel didn't cook.
   (c.) Rachel cooked the meal today so it would be ready for the feast.

3. a. Fruit makes a delicious dessert.
   (b.) Fruit often makes a delicious dessert.
   c. Fruit is dessert.

4. (a.) The kittens purr very loudly when they are sleeping.
   b. The kittens purr.
   c. The kittens purr when they sleep.

5. a. Birds eat seeds.
   b. Birds eat tiny seeds from a feeder.
   (c.) Birds eat many tiny seeds from the feeder in the winter.

6. (a.) The snow falling outside is beautiful.
   b. The snow is beautiful.
   c. The snowballs are cold and sticky.

7. a. Please ask the clerk if they have more berries.
   (b.) Please politely ask the clerk if they have more berries.
   c. Please ask the clerk if they have more fresh berries.

32

Identify It
Circle the adverbs in the following paragraphs. Then, underline the verb, adjective, or other adverb they describe.

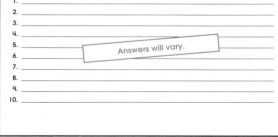

The Emperor's New Clothes, The Snow Queen, and *The Little Mermaid* are just a few fairy tales written by a (remarkably) famous writer. Who so (colorfully) wrote about a little match girl, a brave tin soldier, and an ugly duckling? Hans Christian Andersen did.

Hans Christian Andersen was born (poor) in 1805 in a town in Denmark. What extra money the family had they (eagerly) spent at the theatre. When they didn't have money for tickets, Hans would (quietly) sit (outside) the theatre (actively) reading the playbill. He knew he would (definitely) follow his love of literature and the theatre as a career. With help from grant money, Hans completed school at the University of Copenhagen and became a writer. He wrote (more) than 150 fairy tales. They have been translated into (more) than 100 languages. *The Ugly Duckling,* a tale of self-discovery, was considered by some experts to be an autobiography. Hans also wrote plays, poetry, and travelogues. Hans Christian Andersen remains one of the world's (best) known and (most) translated authors.

Try It
Write ten sentences with at least one adverb in each.

1.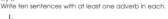
2. _____
3. _____
4. _____
5. _____
6.   Answers will vary.
7. _____
8. _____
9. _____
10. _____

33

Conjunctions are connectors. They connect individual words or groups of words in sentences. There are three kinds of conjunctions.

Coordinate conjunctions connect words, phrases, or clauses, using words like *and, but,* and *or.*

> The snow is cold *and* fluffy.
> Chris likes soccer, *but* Samantha likes football.

Correlative conjunctions are used with pairs and are used together. *Both/and, either/or,* and *neither/nor* are examples of correlative conjunctions.

> *Both* Tammy *and* Tara went to the play. (*Tammy* and *Tara* are a pair.)

Subordinate conjunctions connect two clauses that are not equal. They connect dependent clauses to independent clauses. *After, as long as, since,* and *while* are examples of subordinate conjunctions.

> They run *after* the sun goes down. (dependent clause: *after the sun goes down*)

Complete It
Complete the following sentences with a conjunction from the box.

and	both/and	neither/nor	as long as
but	either/or	after	since

1. Tabitha wanted to have pretzels for a snack _____ **but** _____ Kisha wanted snowcones.
2. _____ **Neither** _____ red _____ **nor** _____ orange was used in the mural.
3. Taylor wanted to go skiing today _____ **since** _____ the big snowfall.
4. Kari didn't go biking _____ **since** _____ it was storming.
5. _____ **Both** _____ Buster _____ **and** _____ Buzz passed puppy training class.
6. Trevor wanted to stay inside and play board games _____ **as long as** _____ it was still raining.
7. _____ **Either** _____ take out the trash _____ **or** _____ walk the dog.
8. We were going to see a movie, _____ **but** _____ we went out to eat, instead.

> More than one answer may be correct. Possible answers given.
> Make sure the given answer is from the correct category of either coordinate, correlative, or subordinate.

34

Identify It
Identify the conjunctions in the following sentences as coordinate, correlative, or subordinate. Write **CD** for coordinate, **CR** for correlative, or **S** for subordinate after each sentence.

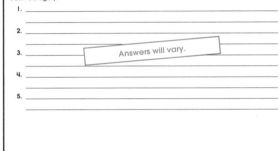

1. **CD** Are we going to go biking or hiking on Saturday?
2. **CR** Neither pasta nor pizza was offered on the menu.
3. **S** As long as it's raining, we may as well get our homework done.
4. **CR** Either Rachel or Carrie will be voted president of the class.
5. **S** Let's walk to school since it is a sunny, warm day.
6. **CD** Todd wants to play baseball this weekend but he has a class in the morning.
7. **S** While we are waiting in line, let's get some popcorn.
8. **CR** Both the girls and the boys' teams are going to the championship.
9. **CD** Grant wants mushrooms and peppers on his pizza.
10. **S** After this week, there's only six weeks of school this year.

Try It
Write five sentences of your own using the conjunctions. Use two conjunctions from each category.

1. _____
2. _____
3. _____ Answers will vary.
4. _____
5. _____

35

An **interjection** is a one- or two-word phrase used to express surprise or strong emotion.

Common interjections:
Ah	Hurray
Aha	Oh
Alas	Ouch
Aw	Uh
Cheers	Uh-huh
Eh	Uh-uh
Hey	Well
Hi	Wow
Huh	Yeah

An exclamation mark is usually used after an interjection to separate it from the rest of the sentence.

> *Oh!* I'm so happy that you can make the trip!

If the feeling isn't quite as strong, a comma is used in place of the exclamation point.

> *Oh,* that's too bad he won't be joining us.

Sometimes question marks are used as an interjection's punctuation.

> *Eh?* Is that really true?

Find It
Use a dictionary to look up each of the following interjections. Write the word's part of speech and the dictionary definition. Then, use each interjection in a sentence.

1. ah - _____
2. alas - _____
3. eh - _____   Answers will vary depending on the dictionary used.
4. hey - _____
5. oh - _____
6. ouch - _____

36

Rewrite It
Carl and Dylan are trying to get a game of backyard baseball started. Rewrite the dialogue to include interjections that will make the passage more lively and fun to read.

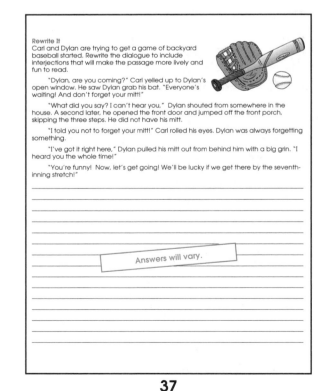

"Dylan, are you coming?" Carl yelled up to Dylan's open window. He saw Dylan grab his bat. "Everyone's waiting! And don't forget your mitt!"

"What did you say? I can't hear you," Dylan shouted from somewhere in the house. A second later, he opened the front door and jumped off the front porch, skipping the three steps. He did not have his mitt.

"I told you not to forget your mitt!" Carl rolled his eyes. Dylan was always forgetting something.

"I've got it right here," Dylan pulled his mitt out from behind him with a big grin. "I heard you the whole time!"

"You're funny! Now, let's get going! We'll be lucky if we get there by the seventh-inning stretch!"

_____
_____
_____
_____
_____
_____

Answers will vary.

_____
_____
_____
_____
_____
_____

37

Prepositions are words or groups of words that show the relationship between a noun or pronoun (the object of the sentence) and another word in the sentence. A prepositional phrase includes the preposition, the object of the preposition, and the modifiers (describes other words) of the object. Prepositional phrases tell about *when* or *where* something is happening.

The students walked **across** *the street*.
(*across* is the preposition; *street* is the object; *across the street* is the prepositional phrase)

The students walked **alongside** *the small park*.
(*alongside* is the preposition; *park* is the object; *small* is the modifier; *alongside the small park* is the prepositional phrase)

Common prepositions:

above	behind	for	over
across	below	from	to
after	beneath	in	toward
along	beside	inside	under
around	between	into	until
at	by	near	up
away	down	off	with
because	during	on	within
before	except	outside	without

Identify It
Identify the preposition, object, and modifier in each of the following sentences. Write a **P** above the preposition, an **O** above the object, and an **M** above the modifier.

                    P   M   O
1. The students played outside at the late recess.

               P   M   O
2. The horse jumped over the high fence.

             P   M   O
3. Alice walked out of the scary movie.

             P   M   O
4. Timmy looked down the deep well.

              P   M   O
5. The paper fell underneath the small bookcase.

38

Solve It
Write a preposition that answers the questions below. Use the list on page 38 if you need help.

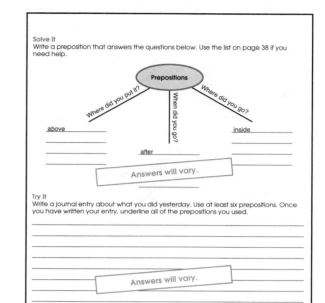

above _____

_____

after _____

inside _____

_____

Answers will vary.

Try It
Write a journal entry about what you did yesterday. Use at least six prepositions. Once you have written your entry, underline all of the prepositions you used.

Answers will vary.

39

Articles are specific words that serve as adjectives before a noun. *A*, *an*, and *the* are articles.

The is a **definite article**. It names a specific noun.
I want to go to *the* park where everyone else went.
(The article *the* shows that the person wants to go to a specific park.)

A and *an* are **indefinite articles**. They do not name a specific noun.
I would like to go to *a* park this weekend.
(The article *a* shows that the person wants to go to any park, and it doesn't matter which one.)

Use *a* when the noun it precedes begins with a consonant or a vowel that sounds like a consonant.
a dress   *a* certificate   *a* book bag   *a* one-way street

Use *an* when the noun it precedes begins with a vowel or vowel sound.
an eyebrow   *an* ostrich   *an* apple   *an* honest person

Match It
Match the object in each set with the article that goes with it. Draw a line from Column A to the correct article in Column B. Then, in Column C, write the article and noun together.

Column A	Column B	Column C
nonspecific play	a	a play
specific play	an	the play
nonspecific envelope	the	an envelope

Column A	Column B	Column C
specific beach	a	the beach
nonspecific beach	an	a beach
nonspecific art piece	the	an art piece

Column A	Column B	Column C
nonspecific hero	a	a hero
nonspecific umbrella	an	an umbrella
specific umbrella	the	the umbrella

40

Proof It
Proofread the following paragraph. Look for mistakes in the use of articles. Use the proof marks to delete incorrect words and insert the correct words.

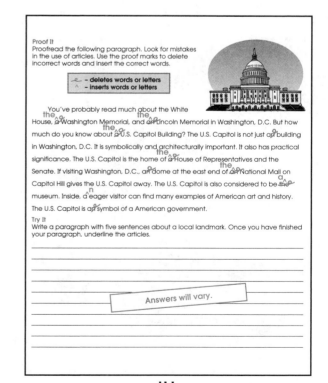

                                           e – deletes words or letters
                                           ∧ – inserts words or letters

You've probably read much about the White House, *a* Washington Memorial, and *an* Lincoln Memorial in Washington, D.C. But how much do you know about *a* U.S. Capitol Building? The U.S. Capitol is not just *an* building in Washington, D.C. It is symbolically and architecturally important. It also has practical significance. The U.S. Capitol is the home of *a* House of Representatives and the Senate. If visiting Washington, D.C., *an* dome at the east end of *an* National Mall on Capitol Hill gives the U.S. Capitol away. The U.S. Capitol is also considered to be *the* museum. Inside, *a* eager visitor can find many examples of American art and history.

The U.S. Capitol is *an* symbol of *a* American government.

Try It
Write a paragraph with five sentences about a local landmark. Once you have finished your paragraph, underline the articles.

Answers will vary.

41

Answer Key

Review: Adjectives, Adverbs

Read each sentence below. When you see **(adj.)**, fill in the blank with an adjective. When you see **(adv.)**, fill in the blank with an adverb.

1. The twins (adv.) _____quietly_____ crept up the stairs.
2. As the children watched, the (adj.) _____furry_____ panda sat down to munch on a stalk of bamboo.
3. Isaiah took a bite of the (adj.) _____spicy_____ soup.
4. The crowd cheered (adv.) _____wildly_____ in the stands.
5. Clementine plucked (adj.) _____golden_____ apples from the trees in the orchard.
6. Both my brothers (adv.) _____eagerly_____ agreed to clean their room in exchange for their allowances.
7. The (adj.) _____cool_____ waves soothed Jack's sunburn.
8. Make sure you drive (adv.) _____carefully_____ on the frozen roads!

Review: Coordinate Conjunctions, Correlative Conjunctions, Subordinate Conjunctions

Circle the conjunction in each sentence. On the line, write whether it is a coordinate, correlative, or subordinate conjunction.

1. The dragonfly (and) the bumblebee circled the flower. _____coordinate_____
2. (Neither) Eddie (nor) Dante has been sick at all this summer. _____correlative_____
3. (Since) Tasha has moved to Oregon, I have not had a best friend. _subordinate_
4. (Both) Chestnut (and) Blaze like to spend the day in the pasture. _____correlative_____
5. (While) her mom is at the library, Minh will play at the park. _____subordinate_____
6. Irina wants to go to the play, (but) Ivan hopes to see a movie. _____coordinate_____

42

Review: Adjectives, Adverbs, Conjunctions, Interjections, Prepositions, Articles

In each sentence, circle the preposition or prepositions. Underline the object of each preposition.

1. Can you imagine living (in) the <u>Arctic</u> and hunting (for) <u>mussels</u> (under) a <u>layer</u> (of) <u>ice</u>?
2. (At) low <u>tide</u>, an Inuit might carve a hole (in) the ocean <u>ice</u>.
3. He can walk (along) the ocean <u>floor</u>.
4. A thick layer (of) <u>ice</u> lies (above) his <u>head</u>.
5. The mussels burrow (below) the <u>sand</u>.
6. The Inuit man places them (inside) his <u>bucket</u>.
7. The sound (of) rushing <u>water</u> is not far.
8. He must hurry back (before) the icy <u>water</u> surrounds him.

Review: Adjectives, Adverbs, Conjunctions, Interjections, Prepositions, Articles

Write the part of speech above the words in bold. Write **ADJ** for adjectives, **ADV** for adverbs, **CONJ** for conjunctions, **INT** for interjections, **PREP** for prepositions, and **ART** for articles.

INT
Hurray! Happy Birthday!

ADV   PREP ADJ   ART   ART
Birthdays were **first** celebrated **in ancient** Rome. **The** Romans celebrated **the**
PREP   ADJ   ADJ   ART   PREP
birthdays **of** their **favorite** gods **and important** people, like **the** emperor. **In** Britain, they
ART ADJ   PREP ART   ART   PREP   CONJ
celebrate **the Queen's** birthday. **In the** United States, **the** birthdays **of** presidents **and**
ADJ   PREP
important leaders, like Martin Luther King, are celebrated. **In**
CONJ   ADJ
Japan, Korea, **and** China, the **sixtieth** birthday marks
ART   PREP ART ADJ   PREP PREP
a transition **from an active** life **to** one **of** contemplation.
ADV ADJ   ART PREP
Many Eastern cultures don't even recognize **the actual** date
PREP   ART ADJ PREP ART ADJ
of birth. When **the first** moon **of the new** year arrives, everyone
ADV ADV
is **one year** older.

43

Declarative sentences are sentences that make statements. They say something about a place, person, thing, or idea. When punctuating a declarative sentence, use a period at the end of the sentence.

    Henry Bergh was the founder of the American Society for the Prevention of Cruelty to Animals.
    Pizza is my favorite food.
    Marathons are 26.2 miles long.

Identify It
Place a check mark in front of each declarative sentence. Leave the other sentences blank.

1. __✓__ Venice is a city in Italy.
2. __✓__ Venice has a network of canals used for transportation.
3. _____ Have you ever been to Venice?
4. __✓__ The Grand Canal is the main thoroughfare.
5. __✓__ Three bridges cross the Grand Canal.
6. _____ How many bridges cross the Grand Canal?
7. _____ Look at the beautiful bridge!
8. __✓__ Venice has a very temperate climate.
9. _____ How warm does it get in Venice in the summer?
10. __✓__ Venice is one of the most beautiful cities in Europe.

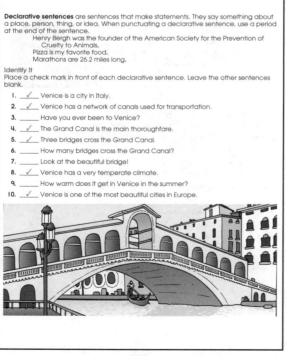

44

Proof It
Make sure that each declarative sentence ends in a period. If the punctuation is correct, place a check mark before the sentence. If not, use the proofreading marks to make each declarative sentence end with a period.

⊙ – inserts period
ℯ – deletes punctuation

1. __✓__ I want to play baseball tomorrow.
2. _____ I can't wait to go to the gym with Greg and Sarah❓⊙
3. __✓__ If you order pizza, make sure to get onions.
4. _____ Do you see the rainbow?
5. _____ Jen said that it is time to eat❓⊙

Try It
Write a dialogue between two people. Write ten sentences about a place they are visiting. Be sure to use periods when you are making declarative sentences.

_____
_____
_____
_____
_____
_____
_____
           Answers will vary.
_____
_____
_____
_____
_____

45

Interrogative sentences are sentences that ask questions. When punctuating an interrogative sentence, use a question mark.

Did I see lightning in the sky**?**
Do you like fresh spinach in your salad**?**
Do you run in the morning or in the evening**?**

Complete It
Complete the following sentences by circling the correct punctuation.

1. Alla walked briskly five times around the block (**.**?)
2. Did you see the famous statue on your vacation (. (**?**)
3. The spider spun a beautiful web (**.**?)
4. Did the poem inspire your artwork (. (**?**)
5. How quickly did you complete the obstacle course (. (**?**)
6. The designer showed great style (**.**?)
7. I like the rhythm of that song (**.**?)
8. Did your dad make spaghetti for dinner last night (. (**?**)
9. Are you going to try out for the wrestling team (. (**?**)
10. Do you lift weights to strengthen your muscles (. (**?**)
11. Are those chestnuts I smell roasting (. (**?**)
12. My friends are coming over after dinner (**.**?)
13. I think the batteries are dead in that radio (**.**?)
14. Aren't the pictures in the museum beautiful (. (**?**)
15. Where are you going after school (. (**?**)
16. Who is at the door (. (**?**)
17. Jon and I walked around the block (**.**?)
18. The baseball game starts at seven o'clock tonight (**.**?)
19. What time did you say (. (**?**)
20. Arlene and Beth joined a book club (**.**?)

46

Solve It
A farmer is taking a student on a tour of his garden. The student has many questions about what kind of vegetables he grows. The farmer's answers are given, but the student's questions are missing. Write the question with the appropriate punctuation in the space provided. The first one has been done for you.

1. How many vegetables do you grow?   I grow many vegetables.
2. What vegetable do you grow the most? I grow mostly soy beans.
3. What is your favorite vegetable?   My favorite vegetable is broccoli.
4. What should I study if I want to be a farmer?   If you want to be a farmer, you should study many subjects, but especially science, math, and social studies.

Try It
Write a list of questions you might ask a local business owner.

Answers will vary.

47

Exclamatory sentences are sentences that reveal urgency, strong surprise, or emotion. When punctuating an exclamatory sentence, use an exclamation mark.

I can't believe you ate the whole pie!
Look at how much weight he is lifting!
I think I smell a skunk!

Only use exclamation points when expressing urgency and strong surprise or emotion. Exclamation marks can also be used in dialogue, when the character or speaker is making an urgent or emotional statement.

Identify It
Identify which sentences are exclamatory by putting an exclamation mark at the end of the sentences. If it's not exclamatory, leave it blank.

1. Watch out for the ice!
2. Ouch! I can't believe I stubbed my toe on the table again!
3. Where are you having dinner tonight
4. The storm is quickly coming our way!
5. I'm not sure if I want to go to the movies or not
6. It is so cold I think I have frostbite!
7. Don't you like the cold weather
8. Ah! The sunset is gorgeous!
9. You're it!
10. Oh no! The bridge is out!
11. What time is it
12. Oranges are my favorite fruit
13. Watch out! The oranges fell off the display!
14. The Lord of the Rings is my favorite series of books!
15. That author really inspires me!

Except for interrogative sentences, answers may be subjective. Accept all reasonable answers.

48

Rewrite It
Read the following postcard from one friend to another. The writer seems excited about her trip, but doesn't express it in her writing. Rewrite the postcard changing declarative sentences to exclamatory ones.

Dear Linda,

I'm having a wonderful time in Florida. The weather is fantastic. It's been sunny every day. We went swimming in the hotel's pool on Tuesday. Then, on Wednesday, we actually swam in the ocean. Tomorrow we are going to visit a marine animal sanctuary. Do you remember studying about the rescued marine animals in school? I can't wait to see the fish and animals. I wish you were here. See you soon.

Drew

Changes are subjective except for the interrogative sentence. Accept all reasonable changes.

Try It
Write a postcard to a friend or relative about a trip you have taken recently. Make it exciting by including exclamatory sentences. Make sentences exclamatory when you really want them to stand out.

Answers will vary.

49

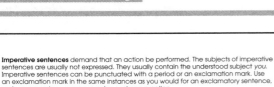

Imperative sentences demand that an action be performed. The subjects of imperative sentences are usually not expressed. They usually contain the understood subject *you*. Imperative sentences can be punctuated with a period or an exclamation mark. Use an exclamation mark in the same instances as you would for an exclamatory sentence, such as expressing urgency, surprise, or strong emotion.

> Look at the rabbit behind the trees.
> (*You* look at the rabbit behind the trees.)
>
> Write the note here.
> (*You* write the note here.)
>
> Throw me the ball!
> (*You* throw me the ball!)

Complete It
Choose a verb from the box that will complete each imperative sentence and write it on the line provided. Remember, the subject *you* is implied in the sentences.

carry	drive	pick	swing	vote
drink	pass	shoot	throw	yell

1. **Vote** for Simon for president!
2. **Pass** the potatoes, please.
3. **Pick** up the paper from the floor.
4. **Carry** that bag for your aunt.
5. **Throw** the ball to second base!
6. **Drive** slowly when on ice.
7. **Swing** the racket higher.
8. **Yell** the cheers louder!
9. **Drink** all of your tomato juice.
10. **Shoot** the basketball through the hoop!

50

Find It
Use a thesaurus to find other imperative words that are synonyms of the imperative words below.

1. call - _____
2. carry - _____
3. drink - _____
4. drive - _____
5. look - _____   *Answers will vary. Accept all reasonable responses.*
6. pass - _____
7. pick - _____
8. run - _____
9. shoot - _____
10. stop - _____

Try It
Write ten imperative sentences using the synonyms from the activity above. Remember to use correct punctuation.

1. _____
2. _____
3. _____
4. _____
5. _____   *Answers will vary.*
6. _____
7. _____
8. _____
9. _____
10. _____

51

Simple sentences are sentences with one independent clause. **Independent clauses** present a complete thought and can stand alone as a sentence. Simple sentences do not have any dependent clauses. **Dependent clauses** do not present a complete thought and cannot stand alone as sentences.

Simple sentences can have one or more subjects.
> The *costumes* glittered.
> The *costumes* and the *jewelry* glittered.

Simple sentences can have one or more **predicates**, or verbs.
> The *costumes* glittered.
> The *costumes* glittered and sparkled.

Simple sentences can have more than one subject and more than one predicate.
> The *costumes* and the *jewelry* glittered and sparkled.

Identify It
Underline the subject or subjects in the following simple sentences.

1. <u>Elsa</u>, Tanya's mom, liked baking cookies.
2. <u>Elsa</u> liked baking cookies and cooking spaghetti.
3. <u>Elsa</u> and <u>Tanya</u> liked baking and cooking together.
4. <u>Elsa</u> liked baking and cooking.
5. <u>Elsa</u> liked baking better.
6. <u>Tanya</u> liked baking and cooking.
7. <u>Tanya</u> liked cooking better.
8. <u>Tanya</u> liked eating her mom's cookies.
9. <u>Elsa</u> liked eating her daughter's spaghetti.
10. <u>Tanya's friends</u> liked coming to dinner.

52

Identify It
Underline the predicate or predicates in the following simple sentences.

1. Elsa, Tanya's mom, <u>liked baking cookies</u>.
2. Elsa <u>liked baking cookies</u> and <u>cooking spaghetti</u>.
3. Elsa and Tanya <u>liked baking</u> and <u>cooking together</u>.
4. Elsa <u>liked baking</u> and <u>cooking</u>.
5. Elsa <u>liked baking better</u>.
6. Tanya <u>liked baking</u> and <u>cooking</u>.
7. Tanya <u>liked cooking better</u>.
8. Tanya <u>liked eating her mom's cookies</u>.
9. Elsa <u>liked eating her daughter's spaghetti</u>.
10. Tanya's friends <u>liked eating cookies and spaghetti</u>.

Try It
Write ten simple sentences of your own. Remember, simple sentences may have more than one subject and more than one predicate.

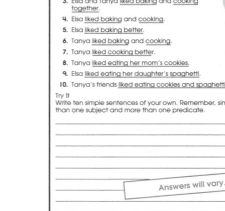

Answers will vary.

53

Answer Key

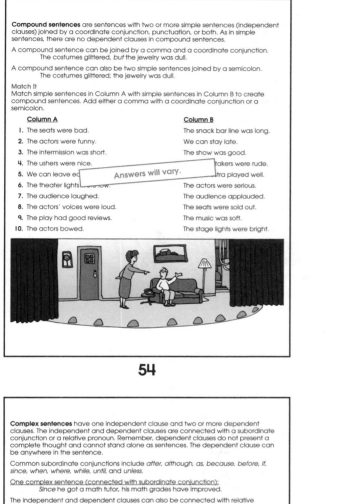

Compound sentences are sentences with two or more simple sentences (independent clauses) joined by a coordinate conjunction, punctuation, or both. As in simple sentences, there are no dependent clauses in compound sentences.

A compound sentence can be joined by a comma and a coordinate conjunction.
The costumes glittered, *but* the jewelry was dull.

A compound sentence can also be two simple sentences joined by a semicolon.
The costumes glittered; the jewelry was dull.

Match It
Match simple sentences in Column A with simple sentences in Column B to create compound sentences. Add either a comma with a coordinate conjunction or a semicolon.

Column A	Column B
1. The seats were bad.	The snack bar line was long.
2. The actors were funny.	We can stay late.
3. The intermission was short.	The show was good.
4. The ushers were nice.	...takers were rude.
5. We can leave e...	...tra played well.
6. The theater lights...	The actors were serious.
7. The audience laughed.	The audience applauded.
8. The actors' voices were loud.	The seats were sold out.
9. The play had good reviews.	The music was soft.
10. The actors bowed.	The stage lights were bright.

Answers will vary.

54

Solve It
Combine each pair of simple sentences into a compound sentence.

Simple Sentences
1. Richard likes apples. Jackie likes pears.
2. Jackie likes skating. Richard likes running.
3. Richard likes dancing. Jackie likes singing.
4. Jackie likes summer. Richard likes winter.
5. Richard likes math. Jackie likes science.

Compound Sentences
1. _____
2. _____
3. _____ *Answers will vary.*
4. _____
5. _____

Try It
Continue to write about what Richard and Jackie each like and don't like. Write three more sentences for each character. Then, combine the sentences to form compound sentences.

Richard
_____ *Answers will vary.*
_____

Jackie
_____ *Answers will vary.*
_____

Compound Sentences
_____ *Answers will vary.*
_____

55

Complex sentences have one independent clause and two or more dependent clauses. The independent and dependent clauses are connected with a subordinate conjunction or a relative pronoun. Remember, dependent clauses do not present a complete thought and cannot stand alone as sentences. The dependent clause can be anywhere in the sentence.

Common subordinate conjunctions include *after, although, as, because, before, if, since, when, where, while, until,* and *unless.*

One complex sentence (connected with subordinate conjunction):
Since he got a math tutor, his math grades have improved.

The independent and dependent clauses can also be connected with relative pronouns like *who, whose, which,* and *that.*

One complex sentence (connected with relative pronoun):
Mr. Addy, *who* is a math teacher, tutors Ashton.

Combining simple sentences into complex sentences adds variety and clarity to writing.

Identify It
Circle the letter that best answers each question.

1. Which of the following contains two simple, individual sentences?
   a. He is wearing his baseball uniform. He is holding his baseball bat.
   b. He is wearing his baseball uniform and holding his baseball bat.
   c. He is wearing his baseball uniform, although the game was cancelled.

2. Which of the following contains a compound sentence?
   a. She is eating a salad. She is drinking lemonade.
   b. She is eating a salad, and she is drinking lemonade.
   c. She is drinking lemonade, since she is thirsty.

3. Which of the following contains a complex sentence?
   a. Mary went jogging. Rose went jogging.
   b. Mary and Rose went jogging.
   c. Before they ate breakfast, Mary and Rose went jogging.

4. Which of the following contains a complex sentence?
   a. Mike was learning about moose at school. Mike was learning about caribou at school.
   b. Mike and Gil were learning about Arctic animals at school.
   c. Mike, who loved animals, was learning about moose and caribou at school.

56

Rewrite It
Rewrite the following article by combining simple sentences to make compound and complex sentences.

Why would a ten-week-old piglet wander the streets of New York City? New York City animal control officers asked the same question. One Friday afternoon they found a tiny piglet. They thought she had escaped from a market. They took her to a shelter. She was treated for wounds on her legs. She was treated for a respiratory infection. The shelter staff named her Priscilla. A local sanctuary took her in. They treated her. She was quite sick. Now she is healthy. Priscilla was adopted by a family in Michigan. She loves her new home.

_____ *Answers will vary.*
_____

Try It
Write an article about an event in your school using compound and complex sentences. Include at least three complex and two compound sentences in your article.

_____ *Answers will vary.*
_____

57

Answer Key

Page 58

Combining short, choppy sentences into longer more detailed sentences makes writing much more interesting and much easier to read. Sentences can be combined in a variety of ways.

<u>Compound subjects and compound verbs:</u>

Brad went on a hiking trip. C.J. went on a hiking trip.
Brad and C.J. went on a hiking trip.

We hiked on our long weekend away. We biked on our long weekend away.
We hiked and biked on our long weekend away.

<u>Adjectives and adverbs:</u>

I ate an orange for breakfast. The orange was sweet.
I ate a *sweet orange* for breakfast.

Abby walked through the foggy forest. Abby walked slowly.
Abby *walked slowly* through the foggy forest.

<u>Making complex sentences (using subordinate conjunctions):</u>

The class was going on a camping trip. They were going on the trip providing it didn't rain.
The class was going on a camping trip *providing it didn't rain.*

Rewrite It
Rewrite these simple sentences into compound or complex sentences.

1. Rachel went to the carnival on Saturday. Dan went to the carnival on Saturday.
   <u>Rachel and Dan went to the carnival on Saturday.</u>

2. The popcorn crackled as it popped. The popcorn snapped as it popped.
   <u>The popcorn crackled and snapped as it popped.</u>

3. Nancy investigated the old trunk. Nancy investigated the brown trunk.
   <u>Nancy investigated the old, brown trunk.</u>

4. Carson excitedly spoke about his journey. Carson loudly spoke about his journey.
   <u>Carson excitedly and loudly spoke about his journey.</u>

5. We can stop for breakfast. We can stop for breakfast if it is quick.
   <u>We can stop for breakfast, as long as it is quick.</u>

58

Page 59

Identify It
Draw a line to match the sentences on the left with the type of combined sentences they are on the right.

1. So that the birthday party remains a surprise, we must get there on time. — complex sentence
2. Helen and Tammy brought sweaters as presents. — compound subjects
3. Helen brought a purple, knit sweater. — combining adjectives

4. Ginger liked raspberry, lemon cake. — combining adjectives
5. Because it was her birthday, Ginger's mom baked her favorite cake. — complex sentence
6. Ginger's mother cooked and baked for hours. — compound verbs

7. Ginger and her friends had a great time at the party. — compound subjects
8. Ginger greatly appreciated the presents. — combining adverbs
9. Although it was late, the friends stayed for more cake. — complex sentence

Try It
Pretend that you are a reporter covering a birthday party. Write an account of the party. Use adjective and adverbs and both compound and complex sentences.

Answers will vary.

59

Page 60

A **sentence fragment** is a group of words that is missing either a subject or a verb. A sentence fragment is also a group of words that doesn't express a complete thought, as in a dependent clause.

Takes a walk every day at lunch. (no subject)
Complete Sentence: *Sandy* takes a walk every day at lunch.

A walk every day at lunch. (no subject and no verb)
Complete Sentence: *Sandy takes* a walk every day at lunch.

Since the line was so long. (not a complete thought)
Complete Sentence: *We went to a different restaurant,* since the line was so long.

Match It
The sentences in Column A are sentence fragments. Choose a group of words from Column B that will complete the sentence and make it whole. Write the new sentences on the line.

Column A	Column B
1. is the twelfth month of the year.	December has two birthstones,
2. Until 46 B.C.,	December
3. Several European countries	Orville Wright made the first heavier-than-air flight at Kitty Hawk, North Carolina,
4. turquoise and zircon.	celebrate December 6th as the Feast of Saint Nicholas.
5. on December 17, 1903.	December had only 29 days.

<u>1. December is the twelfth month of the year.</u>
<u>2. Until 46 B.C., December had only 29 days.</u>
<u>3. Several European countries celebrate December 6th as the Feast of Saint Nicholas.</u>
<u>4. December has two birthstones, turquoise and zircon.</u>
<u>5. Orville Wright made the first heavier-than-air flight at Kitty Hawk, North Carolina, on December 17, 1903.</u>

60

Page 61

Identify It
Now that you have completed the 5 sentences, identify why the sentences in Column A are fragments. Write *missing a subject*, *missing a verb*, or *missing a subject and a verb*.

1. <u>missing a subject</u>
2. <u>missing a subject and a verb</u>
3. <u>missing a verb</u>
4. <u>missing a subject and a verb</u>
5. <u>missing a subject and a verb</u>

Try It
When is your birthday? Write ten complete sentences about the month of your birth. Make sure all of your sentences are complete, with a subject, a verb, and express complete thoughts. Once you have completed your sentences, circle the subjects and underline the verbs.

1. _____
2. _____
3. _____
4. _____
5. _____
6. _____ Answers will vary.
7. _____
8. _____
9. _____
10. _____

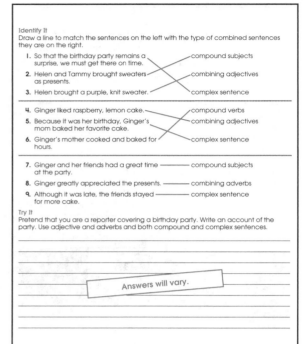

61

Match It
Circle the letter of the best answer in each of the following questions.

1. Which of the following sentences makes the best topic sentence?
   a. Pat was on a journey.
   b. (circled) Pat started on his journey with only his pack on his back.
   c. Pat had a backpack.

2. Which of the following topic sentences is the beginning of a descriptive paragraph?
   a. (circled) The day started out bright and sunny.
   b. School cafeterias should be open before and after school hours.
   c. Building a bookcase can be fast and easy.

3. Which of the following sentences is a sentence from the middle of a paragraph?
   a. A recycling program should be started in our school for three reasons.
   b. (circled) Recycling helps the environment.
   c. Recycling will benefit us all.

4. Which of the following sentences is from a narrative paragraph?
   a. The bears can weigh up to 800 pounds.
   b. Littering is unsanitary and inconsiderate.
   c. (circled) Pat journeyed many days and many nights.

5. Which of the following makes the best concluding sentence?
   a. Charley Babbitt enjoyed painting landscapes.
   b. (circled) Although Charley Babbitt had not set out to become an artist, he grew to love a career that had chosen him.
   c. Charley Babbitt's father wanted him to become a doctor.

6. Which of these sentences is from a persuasive paragraph?
   a. (circled) By turning off the lights when you leave a room, you can save money and electricity every month.
   b. Evan stared at the fender, trying to figure out what had happened.
   c. Ameraucana chickens lay pale blue-green eggs.

7. Which of the following might be the topic of an expository paragraph?
   a. how Queen Annabel escaped from evil Count Rockingham
   b. why Amelia should be allowed to have her own cell phone
   c. (circled) the nesting habits of penguins

63

Rewrite It
The sentences in the following paragraph are out of order. Rewrite the paragraph placing the topic sentence first, the summary sentence last, and the body sentences in between.

He was a quiet man with a personality that drew people to him. He grew up having a close relationship with a tribal chief in South Africa. In his fight to end inequality and seek freedom for all people, Mandela touched millions of lives. Mandela might have become chief one day, but he made a different choice. Nelson Mandela was one of the world's most famous political activists. Mandela's life was one one of many struggles and hardships. He did not follow the easy path in life but chose to work for issues that were important to him. He wanted to change the racial inequalities in his country.

Answers may vary. Possible answer:

Nelson Mandela was one of the world's most famous political activists. He was a quiet man with a personality that drew people to him. He grew up having a close relationship with a tribal chief in South Africa. Mandela might have become chief one day, but he made a different choice. He wanted to change the racial inequalities in his country. Mandela's life had been one of many struggles and hardships. He did not follow the easy path in life but chose to work for issues that were important to him. In his fight to end inequality and seek freedom for all people, Mandela touched millions of lives.

64

Try It
On the lines below, write the rough draft of a descriptive, narrative, expository, or persuasive paragraph. When you are finished, proofread your paragraph carefully. Then, rewrite it including all your edits and changes.

Rough Draft

Final Copy

Answers will vary but should include a rough draft and an edited final copy.

65

Review: Declarative Sentences, Interrogative Sentences, Exclamatory Sentences, Imperative Sentences

Putting It Together
Identify the following sentences. After each sentence, write if the sentence is *declarative, interrogative, exclamatory,* or *imperative.*

1. Walk up the steps and then turn left. __imperative__

2. Anne took a risk and accepted the new job. __declarative__

3. Was that statue priceless? __interrogative__

4. Our team won the game in the final two seconds! __exclamatory__

Review: Simple Sentences, Compound Sentences, Complex Sentences, Sentence Fragments, Combining Sentences

After each sentence, write whether it is a *simple sentence*, a *compound sentence*, a *complex sentence*, or a *sentence fragment*. If the sentences are simple sentences or sentence fragments, rewrite them as compound or complex.

1. Edward wrapped the presents, and Cynthia delivered them. __compound sentence__

2. Although it was a sunny day, __sentence fragment__
   Although it was a sunny day, it was cold outside.

3. The coach challenged her team. The coach inspired her team. __simple sentences__
   The coach challenged her team, and she inspired her team.

4. Grill the peaches until they are slightly brown. __complex sentence__

5. The ocean was blue. The ocean was warm. __simple sentences__
   The ocean was blue, and the ocean was warm.

6. After the hike, __sentence fragment__
   After the hike, we sat down to rest.

Accept any reasonable answer for number 2 and 6.

66

The following paragraph is out of order. Reorder the sentences so they make sense. Rewrite the paragraph and then write what kind of paragraph it is.

It also protects our natural habitats. We should all be committed to a recycling program. The same is true with curbside pollution; less trash means less trash and pollution on our streets. Recycling greatly reduces our need for landfills. It also reduces curbside pollution. When we cut down trees, birds, squirrels, rabbits, and many other forest animals lose their homes. Recycling is important to our environment for many reasons. These are excellent reasons why we should encourage our friends and family to recycle. If we recycle the paper products we use, fewer trees will have to be cut down. Recycling saves trees. If we recycle what would be trash, there will be less garbage to put into the landfills.

Recycling is important to our environment for many reasons. Recycling saves trees. If we recycle the paper products we use, fewer trees will have to be cut down. It also protects our natural habitats. When we cut down trees, birds, squirrels, rabbits, and many other forest animals lose their homes. Recycling greatly reduces our need for landfills. If we recycle what would be trash, there will be less garbage to put into the landfills. It also reduces curbside pollution. The same is true with curbside pollution; less trash means less trash and pollution on our streets. These are excellent reasons why we should encourage our friends and family to recycle. We should all be committed to a recycling program.

Persuasive

67

The names of cities, states, and countries are considered **proper nouns** and are always capitalized.

Capitalize the names of cities:
  Anchorage   Columbus   Kona   Detroit   Los Angeles   New York

Capitalize the names of states:
  Alaska   Ohio   Hawaii   Michigan   California   New York

Capitalize the names of countries:
  United States   Mexico   Japan   Denmark   Israel

Do not capitalize the words *city*, *state*, or *country* in a sentence. These words are common nouns.

Complete It
Circle the correct answer in each of the following sentences.

1. The capital of California is (Sacramento, sacramento).
2. This (City, city) has a population of approximately 407,000.
3. (Los Angeles, los Angeles), has the largest population in California.
4. The city in the United States with the largest population is (New York, new york).
5. The (City, city) of New York has a population of approximately 22 million.
6. The capital city of the state of (New York, new york) is Albany.
7. Albany, (New York, new york) has a population of approximately 40,800.
8. The largest city in (California, california) is Los Angeles.
9. California is the most populated (State, state) in the United States.
10. The least populated state in the United States is (Wyoming, wyoming).
11. China is the most populated (Country, country).
12. The population of (China, china) is over 1.3 billion.
13. The population of the (United States, united States) is over 315 million.
14. The largest continent, Asia, is made up of 48 (Countries, countries).
15. Australia is the only continent that is its own (Country, country).

68

Proof It
Proofread the following journal entry. Use the proofreading marks to correct capitalization errors.

  ≡ – capitalizes a letter
  / – lowercases a letter

  Today was my fourth day in Europe. We have been traveling quickly. I feel like I'm a long way from my home in athens, Ohio. We started our trip in London, england. We saw Big Ben and the Tower of London. Then, we took the tube to paris, france. We climbed the Eiffel Tower—what an awesome view! We also saw the Mona Lisa at The Louvre Museum. France is a beautiful Country. Then, it was off to belgium. We started our tour in the City of Brugges. I have eaten many waffles in ohio, but I've never seen as many as in this Country. Tomorrow we leave belgium for munich, germany. I'm hoping to eat one of those big pretzels while I'm there. I know next year I'm taking an eating tour of Europe.

Try It
Write a journal entry about a city you have visited. Be sure to name the state, if it applies, and the country.

Answers will vary.

69

Days of the week and months of the year are considered **proper nouns** and are always capitalized.

Capitalize days of the week:
  Sunday   Monday   Tuesday   Wednesday   Thursday   Friday   Saturday

Capitalize months of the year:
  January   February   March   April   May   June
  July   August   September   October   November   December

Solve It
The following sentences each contain the name of a day of the week. However, the sentences don't make sense. Unscramble the names of the days of the week so the sentences make sense. Write the day on the line after each sentence. Remember to capitalize the day of the week.

1. dswdeayen falls in the middle of the week. ____Wednesday____
2. The day ryifda got its name from the German word *frigga*. ____Friday____
3. The sun gave its name to nysuda. ____Sunday____
4. hsruydta was named for Thor, a god in northern mythology. ____Thursday____
5. On onmayd, the day of the moon, I go to school. ____Monday____
6. I play baseball on suartyad, the first day of the weekend. ____Saturday____
7. Tiw's day gives its name to usedtay, honoring the northern mythological wrestler Tir. ____Tuesday____

70

Answer Key

Page 75

Solve It
Create your family tree below. Be sure to capitalize proper names. Write three different sentences about the people on this tree.

Answers will vary.

1.
2. Answers will vary. Be sure the names are capitalized
3. correctly depending on how they are used in the sentences.

Try It
What products would you like to invent? Invent some products of your own. Then, give your products an official business name. Come up with at least three business names and three product names. Be sure to capitalize the official business names.

1.
2.
3. Answers will vary.

75

Page 76

Titles are **proper nouns** and are capitalized. The first and last words of titles are always capitalized, as well as every word in between except for articles (*a, an, the*), short prepositions (*in, of, at*), and short conjunctions (*and, but*). These words, however, should be capitalized if they are the first word in the title. Most titles are also underlined in text. Song titles and essays, however, are in quotes.

This rule applies to titles of the following: books, newspapers, magazines, articles, poems, songs, plays, movies, works of art, pictures, stories, and essays.

book: *Catcher in the Rye*   play: *The Music Man*
movie: *Master and Commander*   work of art: *Mona Lisa*

School subjects are capitalized if they name a specific course.
My favorite course is *Literature and Poetry.*

Do not capitalize the names of general subjects.
My *math* teacher is also the baseball coach.

Exception: Language subjects are all proper nouns, so they should all be capitalized.
I am studying my *French* homework.

Complete It
Circle the correct answer that completes each of the following sentences.

1. I read (The Lord of the Rings, the Lord Of The Rings) series during summer vacation.
2. I like doing the crossword puzzle in the (Chicago tribune, Chicago Tribune).
3. My favorite song is ("Drops of Jupiter", "drops of jupiter").
4. Have you ever seen (Raiders of The lost Ark, Raiders of the Lost Ark)?
5. I have gym class after (spanish, Spanish).
6. Mr. Howard is the best (history, History) teacher.
7. Mr. Hayes teaches a course called (Geometry, geometry).
8. Can I walk with you to (Math, math) class?
9. My sister is studying (American poetry, american poetry) in college.
10. The poem ("Dawn", "dawn") by Paul Lawrence Dunbar is one of Dylan's favorites.

76

Page 77

Rewrite It
These reviews have errors in capitalization. Make the corrections as you rewrite them.

* Sleeper of the Year! The movie Happy Times In Snoozeville is for you if you need a nap. The dialogue is boring, the action is slow, and the actors can't act. Don't waste your money on this dud.

* Great Read! The perfect Peach is just what it says—a peach. Take this book to the beach or read it in your favorite armchair. The perfect Peach has rich characters and a comforting mood. Don't miss this great read.

* Ouch! My Ears! What was Kay Joe thinking when she recorded "Dancing in the desert"? She can't hit the high notes and the lyrics make no sense. The track "Singing On The Seas" is worth the money—but buy the single.

Sleeper of the year! The movie Happy Times in Snoozeville is for you if you need a nap. The dialogue is boring, the action is slow, and the actors can't act. Don't waste your money on this dud.

Great read! The Perfect Peach is just what it says - a peach. Take this book to the beach or read it in your favorite armchair. The Perfect Peach has rich characters and a comforting mood. Don't miss this great read.

Ouch! My ears! What was Kay Joe thinking when she recorded "Dancing in the Desert"? She can't hit the high notes and the lyrics make no sense. The track, "Singing on the Seas," is worth the money - but buy the single.

Try It
Write the title of your favorites below. Don't forget to capitalize when necessary and underline or use quotes correctly.

book _____   magazine _____
movie _____   Answers will vary.
song _____   play _____

77

Page 78

The first word of every **sentence** is capitalized.
Build the parfait by sprinkling the berries on the yogurt.

The first word in **direct quotations** is capitalized. Quotation marks are used to show the exact words of a speaker, a direct quotation. The quotation marks are placed before and after the exact words.
Our teacher said, "*Please* go to the board and write your answer."
"*I* hope I know the answer," I whispered as I walked to the board.

Indirect quotations are not capitalized. An indirect quotation does not use the exact words of a speaker and does not use quotation marks.
The coach said he wanted to have practice three nights a week.

If a quotation is split and the second half continues, do not capitalize the second half. If a new sentence begins after the split, then capitalize it as you would with any sentence.
"I think my puppy is the cutest in the class," said the boy, "*and* the best trained."
"My aunt took me to the shelter to get a kitty," said Candy. "*We* found the perfect calico!"

Identify It
One of the sentences in each of the following pairs is not capitalized correctly. Write X on the line before the sentence that is capitalized correctly.

1. __X__ The apartment was perfect for Phyllis and Marc.
   _____ the apartment was perfect for Phyllis and Marc.
2. __X__ "Check out the exercise room," said Maria. "It has everything we use."
   _____ "Check out the exercise room," said Maria. "it has everything we use."
3. _____ The agent John said The pool will open in the spring.
   __X__ The agent John said the pool will open in the spring.
4. __X__ "Rob," said Regina, "the view is fantastic!"
   _____ "Rob," said Regina, "The view is fantastic!"
5. _____ Eddy and Jackie decided They would move next month.
   __X__ Eddy and Jackie decided they would move next month.

78

Answer Key

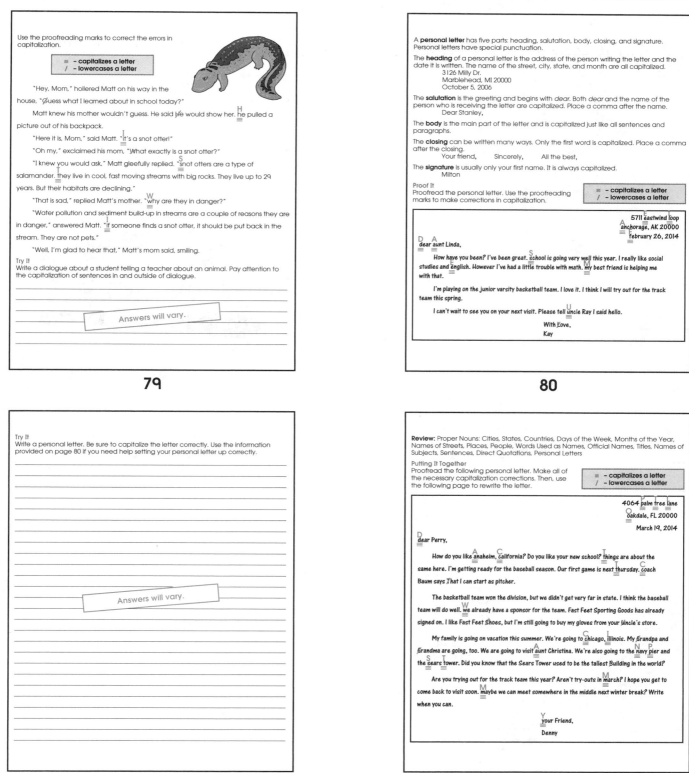

Page 79

Use the proofreading marks to correct the errors in capitalization.

≡ – capitalizes a letter
/ – lowercases a letter

"Hey, Mom," hollered Matt on his way in the house, "Ḡuess what I learned about in school today?"

Matt knew his mother wouldn't guess. He said ḫe would show her. ḫe pulled a picture out of his backpack.

"Here it is, Mom," said Matt. "Ḭt's a snot otter!"

"Oh my," exclaimed his mom, "Ẉhat exactly is a snot otter?"

"I knew you would ask," Matt gleefully replied. "Ṣnot otters are a type of salamander. ṭhey live in cool, fast moving streams with big rocks. They live up to 29 years. But their habitats are declining."

"That is sad," replied Matt's mother. "Ẉhy are they in danger?"

"Water pollution and sediment build-up in streams are a couple of reasons they are in danger," answered Matt. "Ḭf someone finds a snot otter, it should be put back in the stream. They are not pets."

"Well, I'm glad to hear that," Matt's mom said, smiling.

Try It
Write a dialogue about a student telling a teacher about an animal. Pay attention to the capitalization of sentences in and outside of dialogue.

Answers will vary.

79

Page 80

A **personal letter** has five parts: heading, salutation, body, closing, and signature. Personal letters have special punctuation.

The **heading** of a personal letter is the address of the person writing the letter and the date it is written. The name of the street, city, state, and month are all capitalized.
3126 Milly Dr.
Marblehead, MI 20000
October 5, 2006

The **salutation** is the greeting and begins with *dear*. Both *dear* and the name of the person who is receiving the letter are capitalized. Place a comma after the name.
Dear Stanley,

The **body** is the main part of the letter and is capitalized just like all sentences and paragraphs.

The **closing** can be written many ways. Only the first word is capitalized. Place a comma after the closing.
Your friend,   Sincerely,   All the best,

The **signature** is usually only your first name. It is always capitalized.
Milton

Proof It
Proofread the personal letter. Use the proofreading marks to make corrections in capitalization.

≡ – capitalizes a letter
/ – lowercases a letter

5711 ḛastwind ḽoop
ḁnchorage, AK 20000
ḟebruary 26, 2014

ḏear ḁunt Linda,

How have you been? I've been great. Ṣchool is going very well this year. I really like social studies and ḛnglish. However I've had a little trouble with math. Ṃy best friend is helping me with that.

I'm playing on the junior varsity basketball team. I love it. I think I will try out for the track team this spring.

I can't wait to see you on your next visit. Please tell ṵncle Ray I said hello.

With Ḽove,
Kay

80

Page 81

Try It
Write a personal letter. Be sure to capitalize the letter correctly. Use the information provided on page 80 if you need help setting your personal letter up correctly.

Answers will vary.

81

Page 82

Review: Proper Nouns: Cities, States, Countries, Days of the Week, Months of the Year, Names of Streets, Places, People, Words Used as Names, Official Names, Titles, Names of Subjects, Sentences, Direct Quotations, Personal Letters

Putting It Together
Proofread the following personal letter. Make all of the necessary capitalization corrections. Then, use the following page to rewrite the letter.

≡ – capitalizes a letter
/ – lowercases a letter

4064 ṗalm ṭree ḽane
ḟakdale, FL 20000
March 19, 2014

ḏear Perry,

How do you like ḁnaheim, Ḉalifornia? Do you like your new school? Ṭhings are about the same here. I'm getting ready for the baseball season. Our first game is next ṭhursday. Ḉoach Baum says Ṭhat I can start as pitcher.

The basketball team won the division, but we didn't get very far in state. I think the baseball team will do well. Ẉe already have a sponsor for the team. Fast Feet Sporting Goods has already signed on. I like Fast Feet Ṣhoes, but I'm still going to buy my gloves from your ṵncle's store.

My family is going on vacation this summer. We're going to Chicago, Ḭllinois. My Ḡrandpa and Ḡrandma are going, too. We are going to visit ḁunt Christina. We're also going to the ṋavy pier and the ṣears ṭower. Did you know that the Sears Tower used to be the tallest Ḇuilding in the world?

Are you trying out for the track team this year? Aren't try-outs in ṃarch? I hope you get to come back to visit soon. Ṃaybe we can meet somewhere in the middle next winter break? Write when you can.

Ẏour Friend,
Denny

82

_____

Answers will vary.

83

Declarative and imperative sentences both use **periods**. A declarative sentence makes a statement. An imperative sentence demands an action be performed, and the subject is usually not expressed. Sometimes, an imperative sentence can end with an exclamation point.

They left for their trip on Friday.

Look at the icicle formations on the roof!

Quotation marks are used to set off direct quotations in dialogue. Quotation marks are placed before and after the direct quotation. A period is placed at the end of a direct quotation sentence when it is declarative or imperative. The period goes inside the quotation mark.

Lori said, "I'll give the ticket to the agent."

In direct quotation sentences when the quote comes at the beginning of the sentence, use a comma at the end of the direct quotation instead of a period.

"I'll give the ticket to the agent," said Lori.

Complete It

Add the correct punctuation mark in each sentence.

1. "My house is on the right _._" said Martha.

2. Martha said _,_ "My house is on the right."

3. "Look at the bright plants my mom planted _._"

4. "My house has plants like that _._" Deidre replied.

5. Deidre continued, "We also have some bushes mixed in, too _._"

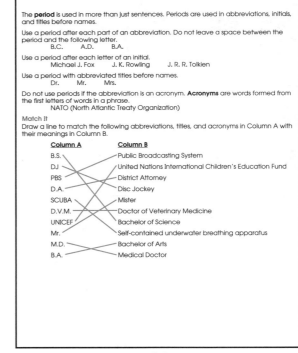

84

Imperative Sentences, In Dialogue

Proof It
Proofread the following paragraphs.
Use proofreading marks to make punctuation corrections.

> ℓ - deletes letters, words, punctuation
> ^ - inserts letters, words, punctuation

"Cities, like cats, reveal themselves at night," said the British poet Rupert Brooke. Perhaps he didn't realize how true his statement is. Some cats save their owners' lives when they reveal themselves at night.

Take, for example, Aggie. Aggie was a cat rescued from a shelter when she was five weeks old. Aggie was curious and playful, but not aggressive. That is until one evening when she heard an intruder trying to climb through the front window. Before her owners even made it downstairs, she pounced, attacked, and scared away the intruder.

Cats also rescue and save their own. One particular cat lived in an abandoned building with her five recently born kittens. When the building caught on fire, what was she to do? Of course she had to save her family. One by one she carried her kittens out of the burning building to safety. She was burned and blistered but she got every one of her kittens out. The firefighter who made sure the cat and kittens were safe and cared for is now known as "The Animal Guy."

Try It
Interview a friend about his or her pet. Then, write a newspaper article about it. Be sure to include direct quotations.

Answers will vary.

_____

The **period** is used in more than just sentences. Periods are used in abbreviations, initials, and titles before names.

Use a period after each part of an abbreviation. Do not leave a space between the period and the following letter.

B.C.   A.D.   B.A.

Use a period after each letter of an initial.

Michael J. Fox   J. K. Rowling   J. R. R. Tolkien

Use a period with abbreviated titles before names.

Dr.   Mr.   Mrs.

Do not use periods if the abbreviation is an acronym. **Acronyms** are words formed from the first letters of words in a phrase.

NATO (North Atlantic Treaty Organization)

Match It

Draw a line to match the following abbreviations, titles, and acronyms in Column A with their meanings in Column B.

Column A	Column B
B.S.	Public Broadcasting System
DJ	United Nations International Children's Education Fund
PBS	District Attorney
D.A.	Disc Jockey
SCUBA	Mister
D.V.M.	Doctor of Veterinary Medicine
UNICEF	Bachelor of Science
Mr.	Self-contained underwater breathing apparatus
M.D.	Bachelor of Arts
B.A.	Medical Doctor

86

Answer Key

Rewrite It
The following people were either misidentified or are not pleased with how their names appeared in a recent magazine article. Rewrite them as they request.

1. Donna Kay Dell — "I prefer my middle name to be an initial."
   Donna K. Dell

2. Melissa Sarah Oliver — "I prefer first and middle initials."
   M. S. Oliver

3. Dr. E. Bates, Ph.D. — "I am a medical doctor."
   Dr. E. Bates, M.D.

4. M. L. Roberts — "I am a doctor."
   Dr. M. L. Roberts, M.D.

5. Steven Paul Starks — "I would like my first name as an initial."
   S. Paul Starks

Try It
You are having a formal party. Make a formal list of ten people you would like to invite. Include their titles and abbreviations, like Mr., Dr., Mrs., and M.D.

Answers will vary.

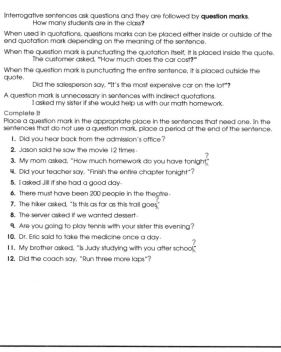

87

Interrogative sentences ask questions and they are followed by **question marks**.
How many students are in the class?

When used in quotations, questions marks can be placed either inside or outside of the end quotation mark depending on the meaning of the sentence.

When the question mark is punctuating the quotation itself, it is placed inside the quote.
The customer asked, "How much does the car cost?"

When the question mark is punctuating the entire sentence, it is placed outside the quote.
Did the salesperson say, "It's the most expensive car on the lot"?

A question mark is unnecessary in sentences with indirect quotations.
I asked my sister if she would help us with our math homework.

Complete It
Place a question mark in the appropriate place in the sentences that need one. In the sentences that do not use a question mark, place a period at the end of the sentence.

1. Did you hear back from the admission's office?
2. Jason said he saw the movie 12 times.
3. My mom asked, "How much homework do you have tonight?"
4. Did your teacher say, "Finish the entire chapter tonight"?
5. I asked Jill if she had a good day.
6. There must have been 200 people in the theatre.
7. The hiker asked, "Is this as far as this trail goes?"
8. The server asked if we wanted dessert.
9. Are you going to play tennis with your sister this evening?
10. Dr. Eric said to take the medicine once a day.
11. My brother asked, "Is Judy studying with you after school?"
12. Did the coach say, "Run three more laps"?

88

Proof It
Proofread the following dialogue. Make corrections using proofreading marks. Look for errors with question mark use.

> ℓ — deletes letters, words, punctuation
> ∧ — inserts letters, words, punctuation
> ↶ — moves punctuation from one place to another

Patrick was doing a report on the Milky Way Galaxy. He asked the director of the local observatory if he could ask him some questions?

Patrick asked, "How many planets orbit the sun in our solar system?"

The director answered, "We have eight planets that orbit the sun."

Patrick asked, "Was my teacher right when she said planets are divided into two categories?"

"Yes, Patrick, Mrs. Sanchez was right," said the director. "Mercury, Venus, Earth, and Mars belong to the terrestrial planets." The director asked, "Do you know the name of the other category?"

"The other category is the Jovian planets," answered Patrick.

The director said, "You are correct!"

Patrick had a good time and learned a lot about the Milky Way Galaxy. He asked the director if he could come back again?

Try It
Choose a subject you would like to know more about. Write a dialogue between you and your teacher. Ask your teacher questions about the subject you chose. Have your teacher ask you questions in the dialogue, too.

Answers will vary.

89

Exclamatory sentences are sentences that express surprise and strong emotion and are punctuated with **exclamation points**.
I'm so excited you made it into the first college on your list!

Interjections sometimes require exclamation points.
Oh, no! I left my homework at home!

Identify It
Identify which sentences should have exclamation points. Place an **X** at the end of each sentence that needs an exclamation point.

1. Watch out! The stove is hot   _X_
2. The soup should be on medium high   _____
3. Thank you for my beautiful flowers   _X_
4. Tulips are my favorite flower   _____
5. Ouch! My fingers were still in the door   _X_
6. After all my hard work, I finally got an A on the test   _X_
7. I have a lot of homework to do tonight   _____
8. I won the race   _X_
9. Oh, no! The rain is coming down really hard now   _X_
10. I like the sound of rain on the rooftop   _____
11. The cars are coming fast   _X_
12. My favorite color is green   _____
13. The ice is slippery   _X_
14. Don't shut the door before getting your keys   _____
15. Wait! I forgot the keys   _X_

90

Answer Key

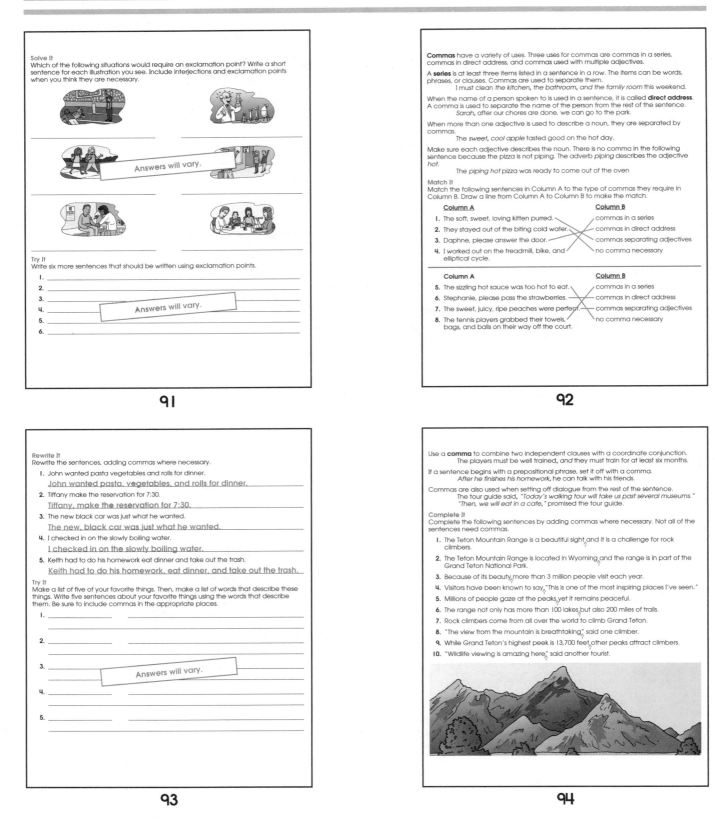

Page 91

Solve It

Which of the following situations would require an exclamation point? Write a short sentence for each illustration you see. Include interjections and exclamation points when you think they are necessary.

Answers will vary.

Try It

Write six more sentences that should be written using exclamation points.

1. _____
2. _____
3. _____
4. _____ Answers will vary.
5. _____
6. _____

Page 92

Commas have a variety of uses. Three uses for commas are commas in a series, commas in direct address, and commas used with multiple adjectives.

A **series** is at least three items listed in a sentence in a row. The items can be words, phrases, or clauses. Commas are used to separate them.
   I must clean *the kitchen, the bathroom, and the family room* this weekend.

When the name of a person spoken to is used in a sentence, it is called **direct address**. A comma is used to separate the name of the person from the rest of the sentence.
   Sarah, after our chores are done, we can go to the park.

When more than one adjective is used to describe a noun, they are separated by commas.
   The *sweet, cool apple* tasted good on the hot day.

Make sure each adjective describes the noun. There is no comma in the following sentence because the pizza is not piping. The adverb *piping* describes the adjective *hot*.
   The *piping hot* pizza was ready to come out of the oven

Match It

Match the following sentences in Column A to the type of commas they require in Column B. Draw a line from Column A to Column B to make the match.

Column A	Column B
1. The soft, sweet, loving kitten purred.	commas in a series
2. They stayed out of the biting cold water.	commas in direct address
3. Daphne, please answer the door.	commas separating adjectives
4. I worked out on the treadmill, bike, and elliptical cycle.	no comma necessary

Column A	Column B
5. The sizzling hot sauce was too hot to eat.	commas in a series
6. Stephanie, please pass the strawberries.	commas in direct address
7. The sweet, juicy, ripe peaches were perfect.	commas separating adjectives
8. The tennis players grabbed their towels, bags, and balls on their way off the court.	no comma necessary

Page 93

Rewrite It

Rewrite the sentences, adding commas where necessary.

1. John wanted pasta vegetables and rolls for dinner.
   John wanted pasta, vegetables, and rolls for dinner.
2. Tiffany make the reservation for 7:30.
   Tiffany, make the reservation for 7:30.
3. The new black car was just what he wanted.
   The new, black car was just what he wanted.
4. I checked in on the slowly boiling water.
   I checked in on the slowly boiling water.
5. Keith had to do his homework eat dinner and take out the trash.
   Keith had to do his homework, eat dinner, and take out the trash.

Try It

Make a list of five of your favorite things. Then, make a list of words that describe these things. Write five sentences about your favorite things using the words that describe them. Be sure to include commas in the appropriate places.

1. _____ _____
2. _____ _____
3. _____ Answers will vary.
4. _____ _____
5. _____ _____

Page 94

Use a **comma** to combine two independent clauses with a coordinate conjunction.
   The players must be well trained, *and* they must train for at least six months.

If a sentence begins with a prepositional phrase, set it off with a comma.
   After he finishes his homework, he can talk with his friends.

Commas are also used when setting off dialogue from the rest of the sentence.
   The tour guide said, *"Today's walking tour will take us past several museums."*
   "Then, we will eat in a cafe," promised the tour guide.

Complete It

Complete the following sentences by adding commas where necessary. Not all of the sentences need commas.

1. The Teton Mountain Range is a beautiful sight, and it is a challenge for rock climbers.
2. The Teton Mountain Range is located in Wyoming, and the range is in part of the Grand Teton National Park.
3. Because of its beauty, more than 3 million people visit each year.
4. Visitors have been known to say, "This is one of the most inspiring places I've seen."
5. Millions of people gaze at the peaks, yet it remains peaceful.
6. The range not only has more than 100 lakes, but also 200 miles of trails.
7. Rock climbers come from all over the world to climb Grand Teton.
8. "The view from the mountain is breathtaking," said one climber.
9. While Grand Teton's highest peak is 13,700 feet, other peaks attract climbers.
10. "Wildlife viewing is amazing here," said another tourist.

Proof It
Proofread the following paragraph. Add commas where necessary.

> ⌐ – deletes letters, words, punctuation
> ^ – inserts letters, words, punctuation

What is a marathon? Most runners know that a marathon is a foot race of 26.2 miles͵but not everyone knows how the marathon began. Now popular worldwide͵the marathon has its roots in Greece. We are familiar with bicycle couriers͵but ancient Greeks used foot couriers. Many of them had to run city to city to make deliveries. In 490 B.C.͵Persia was at war with Greece. A Persian army landed 25 miles from Athens at the city of Marathon. After a mighty battle͵the Greeks were victorious. A runner was sent from Marathon to Athens to spread the news of the victory. Pheidippides ran the 25 miles from Marathon to Athens. When he reached the city͵legend says he said͵ "Rejoice, we conquer." Then, Pheidippides fell dead. Although the facts are not known for sure͵the legend prevails. The modern race got a name͵and the marathon was born.

Try It
Write a paragraph explaining your favorite sport, how it got its beginning, and why you like it. Use a variety of sentences. Add a quotation of your own.

> Answers will vary.

95

The five parts of the personal letter are: **heading**, **salutation (greeting)**, **body**, **closing**, and **signature**. **Commas** appear in four of the five parts of the personal letter.

A **comma** follows the city and the date in the heading.
> 3151 Stuckey Lane
> Chicago, IL 30000
> March 7, 2008

A **comma** follows the name in the salutation.
> Dear Mary,

Follow the normal rules for using comma in sentences.

A **comma** follows the last word in the closing.
> Your friend,

> ↑ – inserts commas

Proof It
Proof the following friendly letter. Add commas where necessary.

> 5512 Alpine Lane
> Ridgeview͵CO 55214
> April 26͵2015
>
> Dear Marina͵
>
> How are you? Are you getting excited for summer? I am going to volunteer at the local animal shelter͵and I am going to learn all about the different kinds of animals there. I am sure that it will be a hard job͵but it will be rewarding, too.
>
> What are your plans for summer? Will you be going camping with your parents like you did last year? That sounds like so much fun! After you get back͵I want to know all about it.
>
> I need to get back to reading about animal care͵and I hope to hear from you soon!
>
> Your friend͵
>
> Sharon

96

Try It
Write a friendly letter of your own. Pay attention to your use of commas.

> Answers will vary.

97

Quotation marks are used to show the exact words of a speaker, called a **direct quotation**. The quotation marks are placed before and after the exact words.
> "I must make it to the post office before 5:00," said Sharon. "I want to get my invitations in the mail today."

Quotation marks are also used when a direct quotation is made within a direct quotation. In this case, single quotation marks are used to set off the inside quotation.
> Dylan said, "Michael, the coach said, 'Practice will be at 4:00 instead of 3:00.'"

The single quotation marks express what the coach said. The double quotation marks express what Dylan is saying as a direct quote.

Quotation marks are used with some titles. Quotation marks are used with the titles of short stories, poems, songs, and articles in magazines and newspapers.
> short story: "*A White Heron*"

If a title is quoted within a direct quotation, then single quotation marks are used.
> Hannah said, "I hope the DJ plays my favorite song, 'Purple People Eater.'"

Match It
Match the following sentences or titles from Column A to the type of quotation in Column B. Draw a line to make the match.

Column A	Column B
1. Susan said, "Let's go to lunch at 12:30."	direct quotation
2. Connie answered, "My boss said, 'Our lunch meeting is scheduled for 12:00 sharp.'"	quote within a quote
3. "Prairie Island"	title

Column A	Column B
4. "Soak Up the Sun"	direct quotation
5. My sister said, "The coach said 'Eat a good dinner thenight before the game.'"	quote within a quote
6. "I'm heading for the beach," Sheryl said.	title

98

Answer Key

Page 99

Proof It
Proofread the following dialogue using proofreading marks. Make corrections on the use of quotation marks.

| ⯗ – inserts quotations |

"Claude Monet lived from 1840 to 1926. He was the founder of impressionism," said Mrs. Konikow.

"What is impressionism?" asked Doug.

"Impressionism is an art form that captures a visual image and uses colors to give the effect of reflected light. Many of Monet's paintings were landscapes," answered Mrs. Konikow.

"Did Mrs. Konikow say, 'Many of Monet's paintings were landscapes?'" asked Patricia.

"Yes," answered Doug, "landscapes are stretches of scenery that can be seen in one view."

"Like flower gardens?" asked Patricia.

"Yes, Patricia," said Mrs. Konikow, "like flower gardens. Later in his life, Monet retired from Paris and moved to his home in Giverny, France, where he continued to paint. He had beautiful gardens. You can see them in books and at his house in France."

"Someday, I would like to go to France," said Patricia, "but for now I think I'll just take a trip to the library."

Try It
Practice writing sentences with quotation marks. Write one sentence that is a direct quotation, one that is a quote within quotes, and one that includes a title.

1. _____
2. _____ Answers will vary. _____
3. _____

99

Page 100

Apostrophes are used to form contractions, possessives, and plurals.

Contractions are shortened forms of words. The words are shorted by leaving out letters. An apostrophe takes the place of the omitted letters.
  I am = I'm   let us = let's

Possessives show possession, or ownership. To form the possessive of a singular noun, add an apostrophe and an **s**.
  I have *Walt's* books.

To form the possessive of plural nouns ending in **s**, simply add the apostrophe. If the plural noun does not end in an **s**, add both the apostrophe and an **s**.
  The *boys'* uniforms will be ready on Friday.
  The *children's* puppet show will be performed on Wednesday.

If you are writing about more than one letter of the alphabet or number, only add **s** to form the plural.
  My name has two B**s** in it.
  I have two page 4**s** in my book.

Complete It
Complete the following sentences by changing words to contractions. Write the contraction on the line that follows the words.

| We're | It's | He'd |
| I'm | We've | let's |

1. (I am) _____ I'm _____ hungry and thirsty.
2. (We are) _____ We're _____ on our way to the café.
3. (It is) _____ It's _____ not too far away, and it has the best muffins.
4. Do you think we should take something back for Pablo? (He would) _____ He'd _____ appreciate it.
5. (We have) _____ We've _____ a lot of homework to do at lunch.
6. Come on, (let us) _____ let's _____ hurry.

100

Page 101

Solve It
Look at the pictures below and write a sentence for each that identifies the object and who the object belongs to. The first one has been done for you.

1. The ___ Answers will vary. ___
2. The kitty's treats are in a foil bag.
3. The runners' shoes are muddy.
4. The chef's vegetables are fresh.
5. The tourists' map is big.

Try It
Write how many letters are duplicated in the following names. Then, on the last line, write your name. Write how many letters are duplicated in your name. The first one has been done for you.

1. Nathan *2 Ns and 2 As*
2. Lee _2 Es_
3. Greg _2 Gs_
4. McKenna _2 Ns_
5. David _2 Ds_
6. ___ Answers will vary. ___

101

Page 102

Colons are used to introduce a series, to set off a clause, for emphasis, and in time.

Colons are used to introduce a series in a sentence. Usually, but not always, the list is proceeded by the words *following, these, things*.
  The chef does the *following*: washes the vegetables, chops the vegetables, and steams the vegetables.

Colons are sometimes used instead of a comma, in more formal cases, to set off a clause.
  The weather reporter said: *"We can expect six more inches of snow overnight."*

Colons are used to set off a word or phrase for emphasis.
  We hoped to see some activity in the night sky. And then we saw it: *a shooting star.*

Colons are used when writing the time.
  Are we meeting at 9:00 or 10:00?

Identify It
Identify why the colon is used in each sentence. Write a **S** for series, **C** for clause, **E** for emphasis, or **T** for time.

1. _E_ One of the most violent storms occurs primarily in the United States: tornados.
2. _C_ A tornado is defined as the following: "a violent rotating column of air extending from a thunderstorm to the ground."
3. _S_ Thunderstorms that develop in warm, moist air in advance of a cold front can produce these things: hail, strong wind, and tornados.
4. _T_ Tornados are most likely to occur in the spring and summer months between 3:00 pm and 9:00 pm, but can occur anytime.
5. _S_ Staying aware is most important for safety. During storms, look for the following: dark, greenish skies, large hail, loud roars, and flash floods.
6. _S_ You can be prepared by doing the following: developing a safety plan, practicing house drills, and listening to weather reports.

102

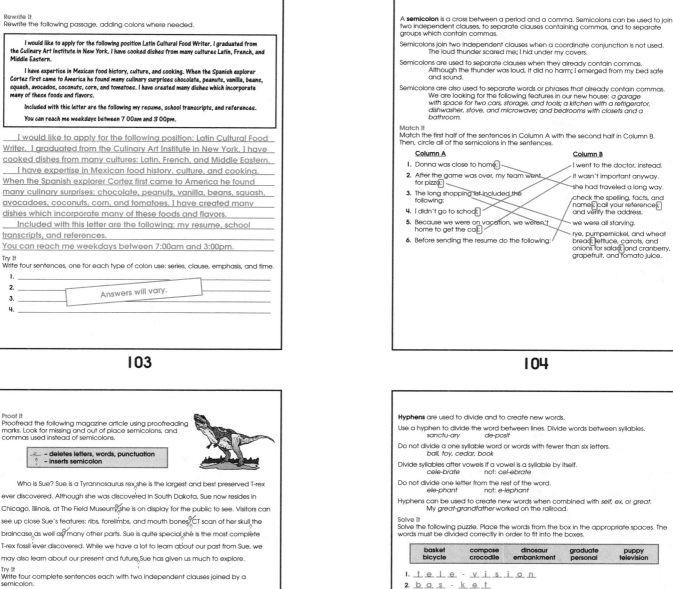

Page 103

Rewrite It
Rewrite the following passage, adding colons where needed.

> I would like to apply for the following position Latin Cultural Food Writer. I graduated from the Culinary Art Institute in New York. I have cooked dishes from many cultures Latin, French, and Middle Eastern.
>
> I have expertise in Mexican food history, culture, and cooking. When the Spanish explorer Cortez first came to America he found many culinary surprises chocolate, peanuts, vanilla, beans, squash, avocados, coconuts, corn, and tomatoes. I have created many dishes which incorporate many of these foods and flavors.
>
> Included with this letter are the following my resume, school transcripts, and references.
>
> You can reach me weekdays between 7 00am and 3 00pm.

I would like to apply for the following position: Latin Cultural Food Writer. I graduated from the Culinary Art Institute in New York. I have cooked dishes from many cultures: Latin, French, and Middle Eastern.
I have expertise in Mexican food history, culture, and cooking. When the Spanish explorer Cortez first came to America he found many culinary surprises: chocolate, peanuts, vanilla, beans, squash, avocadoes, coconuts, corn, and tomatoes. I have created many dishes which incorporate many of these foods and flavors.
Included with this letter are the following: my resume, school transcripts, and references.
You can reach me weekdays between 7:00am and 3:00pm.

Try It
Write four sentences, one for each type of colon use: series, clause, emphasis, and time.

1. _____
2. _____ Answers will vary.
3. _____
4. _____

Page 104

A **semicolon** is a cross between a period and a comma. Semicolons can be used to join two independent clauses, to separate clauses containing commas, and to separate groups which contain commas.

Semicolons join two independent clauses when a coordinate conjunction is not used.
The loud thunder scared me; I hid under my covers.

Semicolons are used to separate clauses when they already contain commas.
Although the thunder was loud, it did no harm; I emerged from my bed safe and sound.

Semicolons are also used to separate words or phrases that already contain commas.
We are looking for the following features in our new house: a garage with space for two cars, storage, and tools; a kitchen with a refrigerator, dishwasher, stove, and microwave; and bedrooms with closets and a bathroom.

Match It
Match the first half of the sentences in Column A with the second half in Column B. Then, circle all of the semicolons in the sentences.

Column A
1. Donna was close to home;
2. After the game was over, my team went for pizza;
3. The long shopping list included the following:
4. I didn't go to school;
5. Because we were on vacation, we weren't home to get the call;
6. Before sending the resume do the following:

Column B
I went to the doctor, instead.
it wasn't important anyway.
she had traveled a long way.
check the spelling, facts, and names; call your references; and verify the address.
we were all starving.
rye, pumpernickel, and wheat bread; lettuce, carrots, and onions for salad; and cranberry, grapefruit, and tomato juice.

Page 105

Proof It
Proofread the following magazine article using proofreading marks. Look for missing and out of place semicolons, and commas used instead of semicolons.

- – deletes letters, words, punctuation
- – inserts semicolon

Who is Sue? Sue is a Tyrannosaurus rex; she is the largest and best preserved T-rex ever discovered. Although she was discovered in South Dakota, Sue now resides in Chicago, Illinois, at The Field Museum; she is on display for the public to see. Visitors can see up close Sue's features: ribs, forelimbs, and mouth bones; CT scan of her skull, the braincase, as well as many other parts. Sue is quite special; she is the most complete T-rex fossil ever discovered. While we have a lot to learn about our past from Sue, we may also learn about our present and future; Sue has given us much to explore.

Try It
Write four complete sentences each with two independent clauses joined by a semicolon.

Answers will vary.

Page 106

Hyphens are used to divide and to create new words.

Use a hyphen to divide the word between lines. Divide words between syllables.
sanctu-ary   de-posit

Do not divide a one syllable word or words with fewer than six letters.
ball, toy, cedar, book

Divide syllables after vowels if a vowel is a syllable by itself.
cele-brate   not: cel-ebrate

Do not divide one letter from the rest of the word.
ele-phant   not: e-lephant

Hyphens can be used to create new words when combined with self, ex, or great.
My great-grandfather worked on the railroad.

Solve It
Solve the following puzzle. Place the words from the box in the appropriate spaces. The words must be divided correctly in order to fit into the boxes.

basket	compose	dinosaur	graduate	puppy
bicycle	crocodile	embankment	personal	television

1. tele-vision
2. bas-ket
3. per-sonal
4. croco-dile
5. gradu-ate
6. com-pose
7. embank-ment
8. bicy-cle
9. puppy
10. dino-saur

Answer Key

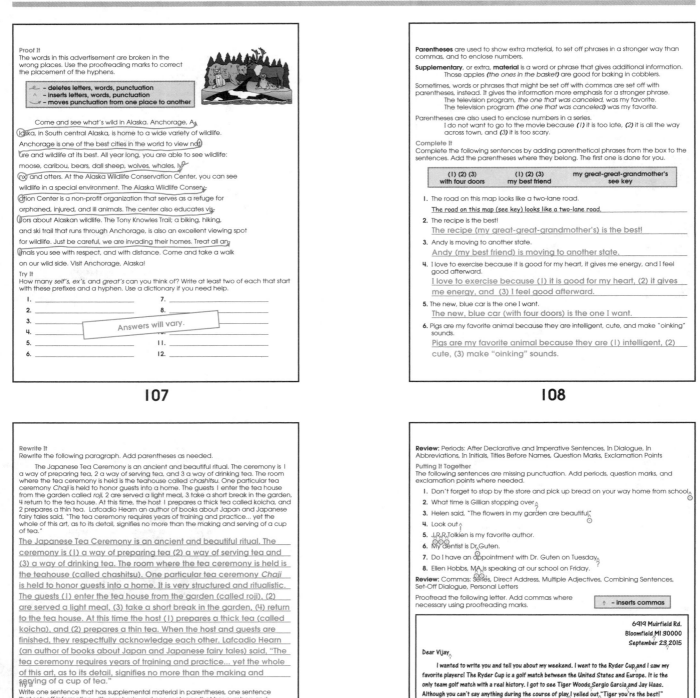

Proof It
The words in this advertisement are broken in the wrong places. Use the proofreading marks to correct the placement of the hyphens.

- ꝰ – deletes letters, words, punctuation
- ∧ – inserts letters, words, punctuation
- ⌒ – moves punctuation from one place to another

    Come and see what's wild in Alaska. Anchorage, A/laska, in South central Alaska, is home to a wide variety of wildlife. Anchorage is one of the best cities in the world to view na/ture and wildlife at its best. All year long, you are able to see wildlife: moose, caribou, bears, dall sheep, wolves, whales, ly/nx and otters. At the Alaska Wildlife Conservation Center, you can see wildlife in a special environment. The Alaska Wildlife Conserv/ation Center is a non-profit organization that serves as a refuge for orphaned, injured, and ill animals. The center also educates vis/itors about Alaskan wildlife. The Tony Knowles Trail; a biking, hiking, and ski trail that runs through Anchorage, is also an excellent viewing spot for wildlife. Just be careful, we are invading their homes. Treat all an/imals you see with respect, and with distance. Come and take a walk on our wild side. Visit Anchorage, Alaska!

Try It
How many *self's*, *ex's*, and *great's* can you think of? Write at least two of each that start with these prefixes and a hyphen. Use a dictionary if you need help.

1. _____ 7. _____
2. _____ 8. _____
3. _____
4. _____ *Answers will vary.*
5. _____ 11. _____
6. _____ 12. _____

107

Parentheses are used to show extra material, to set off phrases in a stronger way than commas, and to enclose numbers.

Supplementary, or extra, **material** is a word or phrase that gives additional information.
    Those apples *(the ones in the basket)* are good for baking in cobblers.

Sometimes, words or phrases that might be set off with commas are set off with parentheses, instead. It gives the information more emphasis for a stronger phrase.
    The television program, *the one that was canceled*, was my favorite.
    The television program *(the one that was canceled)* was my favorite.

Parentheses are also used to enclose numbers in a series.
    I do not want to go to the movie because *(1)* it is too late, *(2)* it is all the way across town, and *(3)* it is too scary.

Complete It
Complete the following sentences by adding parenthetical phrases from the box to the sentences. Add the parentheses where they belong. The first one is done for you.

(1) (2) (3) with four doors	(1) (2) (3) my best friend	my great-great-grandmother's see key

1. The road on this map looks like a two-lane road.
    The road on this map (see key) looks like a two-lane road.
2. The recipe is the best!
    The recipe (my great-great-grandmother's) is the best!
3. Andy is moving to another state.
    Andy (my best friend) is moving to another state.
4. I love to exercise because it is good for my heart, it gives me energy, and I feel good afterward.
    I love to exercise because (1) it is good for my heart, (2) it gives me energy, and (3) I feel good afterward.
5. The new, blue car is the one I want.
    The new, blue car (with four doors) is the one I want.
6. Pigs are my favorite animal because they are intelligent, cute, and make "oinking" sounds.
    Pigs are my favorite animal because they are (1) intelligent, (2) cute, (3) make "oinking" sounds.

108

Rewrite It
Rewrite the following paragraph. Add parentheses as needed.

    The Japanese Tea Ceremony is an ancient and beautiful ritual. The ceremony is 1 a way of preparing tea, 2 a way of serving tea, and 3 a way of drinking tea. The room where the tea ceremony is held is the teahouse called *chashitsu*. One particular tea ceremony *Chaji* is held to honor guests into a home. The guests 1 enter the tea house from the garden called *roji*, 2 are served a light meal, 3 take a short break in the garden, 4 return to the tea house. At this time, the host 1 prepares a thick tea called koicha, and 2 prepares a thin tea. Lafcadio Hearn an author of books about Japan and Japanese fairy tales said, "The tea ceremony requires years of training and practice... yet the whole of this art, as to its detail, signifies no more than the making and serving of a cup of tea."

The Japanese Tea Ceremony is an ancient and beautiful ritual. The ceremony is (1) a way of preparing tea (2) a way of serving tea and (3) a way of drinking tea. The room where the tea ceremony is held is the teahouse (called chashitsu). One particular tea ceremony *Chaji* is held to honor guests into a home. It is very structured and ritualistic. The guests (1) enter the tea house from the garden (called roji), (2) are served a light meal, (3) take a short break in the garden, (4) return to the tea house. At this time the host (1) prepares a thick tea (called koicha), and (2) prepares a thin tea. When the host and guests are finished, they respectfully acknowledge each other. Lafcadio Hearn (an author of books about Japan and Japanese fairy tales) said, "The tea ceremony requires years of training and practice... yet the whole of this art, as to its detail, signifies no more than the making and serving of a cup of tea."

Write one sentence that has supplemental material in parentheses, one sentence that sets off information with emphasis, and one sentence that has numbers and parentheses.

1. _____
2. _____ *Answers will vary.*
3. _____

109

Review: Periods: After Declarative and Imperative Sentences, In Dialogue, In Abbreviations, In Initials, Titles Before Names, Question Marks, Exclamation Points

Putting It Together
The following sentences are missing punctuation. Add periods, question marks, and exclamation points where needed.

1. Don't forget to stop by the store and pick up bread on your way home from school.
2. What time is Gillian stopping over?
3. Helen said, "The flowers in my garden are beautiful."
4. Look out!
5. J.R.R.Tolkien is my favorite author.
6. My dentist is Dr. Guten.
7. Do I have an appointment with Dr. Guten on Tuesday?
8. Ellen Hobbs, MA, is speaking at our school on Friday.

Review: Commas: Series, Direct Address, Multiple Adjectives, Combining Sentences, Set-Off Dialogue, Personal Letters

Proofread the following letter. Add commas where necessary using proofreading marks.

∧ – inserts commas

6919 Muirfield Rd.
Bloomfield, MI 30000
September 23, 2015

Dear Vijay,

    I wanted to write you and tell you about my weekend. I went to the Ryder Cup, and I saw my favorite players! The Ryder Cup is a golf match between the United States and Europe. It is the only team golf match with a real history. I got to see Tiger Woods, Sergio Garcia, and Jay Haas. Although you can't say anything during the course of play, I yelled out, "Tiger, you're the best!" between holes. It was great. I bought you a hat at the gift shop, and I'll give it to you when I see you winter break. I hope you are well.

Your friend,
Mindy

110

Answer Key

Review: Quotation Marks, Apostrophes, Colons, Semicolons, Hyphens, Parentheses

Rewrite each sentence. Add punctuation where necessary.

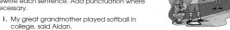

1. My great grandmother played softball in college, said Aidan.

   "My great-grandmother played softball in college," said Aidan.

2. The doctor said "You'll be fine!"

   The doctor said, "You'll be fine!"

3. I want to take Ms. Roses class because 1 she teaches a lot of geography, 2 she takes her classes on field trips, and 3 she is nice.

   I want to take Ms. Rose's class because (1) she teaches a lot of geography, (2) she takes her classes on field trips, and (3) she is nice.

4. "Charlotte, did our teacher say, the bus for the museum leaves at 9 00?"

   "Charlotte, did our teacher say, 'The bus for the museum leaves at 9:00'?"

5. I am excited about going to the museum of art I want to be an artist someday.

   I am excited about going to the museum of art; I want to be an artist someday.

6. Susan got what she had been hoping for a new job.

   Susan got what she had been hoping for: a new job.

7. I didnt read the series, The Lord of the Rings, but I loved the movies.

   I didn't read the series, The Lord of the Rings, but I loved the movies.

111

The **present tense** of a verb tells that the action is taking place now or continuously.
I do the crossword puzzles on Sunday.

The **past tense** of a verb tells that the action took place in the past.
Renee and Kristen went on an archeological dig last semester.

The **past participle** of a verb tells that the action began in the past and was completed in the past. In order to form the past participle, the verb must be preceded by one of the following verbs: *was, were, has, had,* or *have.*
Yuki, Lori, and Blair had come with us on our vacation three years in a row.

Complete It
Complete the following sentences by circling the correct verb in parentheses.

1. Timmy (come, (has come)) over for dinner every night this week.
2. I can (did, (do)) my homework now.
3. The class (go, (had gone)) to the same exhibit last year.
4. Please (came, (come)) and pick up your order.
5. Andrea (do, (has done)) that assignment many times before.
6. The butterflies ((had come,) has come) back to this same location for many years.
7. Bianca and Nicole (gone, (went)) to see the butterflies at the butterfly house.
8. Meg (did, (was done)) with her chores before the programs started.
9. Ollie ((came,) come) home from his vacation with many pictures.
10. Trinity and Eddie ((go,) gone) to the same vet as Eric and Shane.

112

Proof It
Proofread the following paragraph. Use the proofreading marks to correct errors with the use of the verbs *run, see,* and *sit.* Use clues from the rest of the _____ what the tense _____

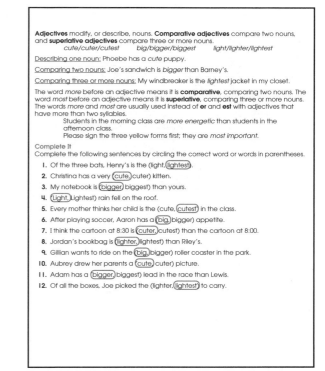

> Answers will vary. Some answers are subjective.
> inserts letters, words, punctuation

They ~~have ran~~, follow, sniff, ~~have sat~~, and sometimes they ~~sit~~. They are an
important member of many teams. Who are they? They are rescue dogs. Rescue dogs are important to police departments, fire departments, and many rescue organizations. Rescue dogs can ~~saw~~ and smell things human beings can't. Human rescuers ~~saw~~ these dogs ~~had run~~ through wildernesses looking for missing persons, sniffing for clues along the way. Some dogs ~~ran~~ up snowy mountains to find fallen hikers and skiers. Sometimes they ~~have sat~~ for hours waiting for their turn to seek and rescue. And when they are called, they are ready to go.

Rescue dogs and their guardians are well trained teams. They work together, ~~ran~~ together, play together, and rescue together. These teams go through many hours of intensive training ~~and see~~ and experienced many types of challenging situations. We owe a lot to these hard-working dogs and those who train and love them.

Many believe that rescue dogs run with their noses to the ground in order to pick up scents. It's not necessarily true; rescue dogs can be trained to receive scents from the air and can ~~ran~~ with noses up!

Try It
Practice writing the present, past, and past participle forms of the verbs *run, see,* and *sit.* Write one sentence of each type for each verb.

> Answers will vary.

113

Adjectives modify, or describe, nouns. **Comparative adjectives** compare two nouns, and **superlative adjectives** compare three or more nouns.
cute/cuter/cutest   big/bigger/biggest   light/lighter/lightest

Describing one noun: Phoebe has a *cute* puppy.

Comparing two nouns: Joe's sandwich is *bigger* than Barney's.

Comparing three or more nouns: My windbreaker is the *lightest* jacket in my closet.

The word **more** before an adjective means it is **comparative**, comparing two nouns. The word **most** before an adjective means it is **superlative**, comparing three or more nouns. The words **more** and **most** are usually used instead of **er** and **est** with adjectives that have more than two syllables.
Students in the morning class are *more energetic* than students in the afternoon class.
Please sign the three yellow forms first; they are *most important.*

Complete It
Complete the following sentences by circling the correct word or words in parentheses.

1. Of the three bats, Henry's is the (light, (lightest)).
2. Christina has a very ((cute,) cuter) kitten.
3. My notebook is ((bigger,) biggest) than yours.
4. ((Light,) Lightest) rain fell on the roof.
5. Every mother thinks her child is the (cute, (cutest)) in the class.
6. After playing soccer, Aaron has a ((big,) bigger) appetite.
7. I think the cartoon at 8:30 is ((cuter,) cutest) than the cartoon at 8:00.
8. Jordan's bookbag is ((lighter,) lightest) than Riley's.
9. Gillian wants to ride on the ((big,) bigger) roller coaster in the park.
10. Aubrey drew her parents a ((cute,) cuter) picture.
11. Adam has a ((bigger,) biggest) lead in the race than Lewis.
12. Of all the boxes, Joe picked the (lighter, (lightest)) to carry.

114

Panel 115

Identify It

Identify each of the following sentences as either a comparative sentence or a superlative sentence. Write **C** for comparative and **S** for superlative. Then, underline the adjectives (including the words *more* or *most*) in the sentences.

1. __S__ The most challenging sports competition in the world is the Tour de France.
2. __S__ The Tour de France can be ridden in some of the worst weather conditions.
3. __S__ One of the best shirts to earn in the Tour de France is the polka-dot jersey.
4. __S__ The world's most famous bicyclers come to France to compete.
5. __C__ Athletes now have more specialized training than they did years ago.
6. __C__ The more training an athlete has, the more prepared they will be.

Try It

Write a paragraph describing a performance or sporting event you have seen. Use at least six comparative or superlative adjectives.

Answers will vary.

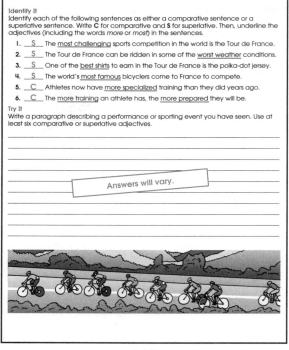

115

Panel 116

Adverbs modify verbs, adjectives, and other adverbs. Some adverbs are easily confused with adjectives.

Bad is an adjective and *badly* is an adverb. Determine what you are modifying before using *bad* and *badly*.

A *bad* storm is heading our way.

Bad is used as an adjective modifying the noun *storm*. No **ly** is added.

Cami sings *badly*.

Badly is used as an adverb modifying the verb *sings*. Use the **ly** form of *bad*.

Good is an adjective and *well* is an adverb. Determine what you are modifying before using *good* and *well*.

Claudia is a *good* cook and bakes *well*, too.

In this sentence, the adverb *well* modifies the verb *bakes*. The adjective *good* modifies the noun *cook*.

The words *very* and *really* are both adverbs.

Please talk *very* softly in the library.

The adverb *very* modifies the adverb *softly* that modifies the verb *talk*.

Complete It

Complete the following sentences by circling the correct adverb in parentheses. Underline the verb, adjective, or adverb that it modifies. Then, write what type of word it modifies: **V** for verb, **ADJ** for adjective, **ADV** for adverb, and **N** for noun.

1. __V__ Jim was sick and so ran (bad, (badly)) during the race.
2. __V__ Amy had a great day and ran (good, (well)) in her race.
3. __N__ The day I lost the race was a ((bad), badly) day for me.
4. __ADJ__ I was a (bad, (badly)) beaten runner.
5. __N__ But it was a ((good), well) day for my friend.
6. __V__ She accepted her praises (good, (well)).
7. __V__ I will train harder so I do (good, (well)) in my next race.
8. __N__ That will be a ((good), well) day for the whole team.

116

Panel 117

Proof It

Proofread the following article using proofreading marks. Look for errors with adjectives and adverbs. When you come to the adverbs *really* or *very*, underline the words they modify.

> ⌐e⌐ – deletes letters, words, punctuation
> ^ – inserts letters, words, punctuation

Where do you go to find the very best in wildlife viewing? The answer varies greatly. Well viewing can be found all over the United States. One particular wildlife refuge is good hidden. The Arctic National Wildlife Refuge is located in northern Alaska on the Bering Strait. You can only reach it by bush plane. But the travel is worth it with well sightings of caribou, wolves, grizzly and black bears, musk oxen, polar bears, and wolverines. The area is known for badly storms. Visit with a good trained guide.

If it is aquatic animals you really want to see, you should go to the Everglades in Florida. If you paddle good and are in well shape, you can canoe or kayak on the water trails. Visit in January or February, or you may be bad bitten by mosquitoes. Those who visit are really excited to see alligators, dolphins, crocodiles, flamingos, and manatees. From Alaska to Florida and many places in between, well wildlife viewing is there for you to see.

Try It

Write an article describing a school event in which some things went well, and some things didn't go so well. Use each of the words *bad, badly, good, well, really,* and *very* at least once.

Answers will vary.

117

Panel 118

A **negative** sentence states the opposite. Negative words include: *not, no, never, nobody, nowhere, nothing, barely, hardly, scarcely,* and contractions containing the word *not.*

Double negatives occur when two negative words are used in the same sentence. Don't use double negatives; it will make your sentence positive again, and it is poor grammar.

> Negative: We do *not* have any soup in the pantry.
> Double negative: We do *not* have *no* soup in the pantry.

> Negative: I have *nothing* to wear to the party this weekend.
> Double negative: I *don't* have *nothing* to wear to the party this weekend.

> Negative: Greg can *hardly* put weight on his leg since his knee operation.
> Double negative: Greg *can't hardly* put weight on his leg since his knee operation.

Identify It

Identify which of the following sentences have double negatives by writing an **X** on the lines. Then, go back and correct the double negatives by crossing out one of the negatives or by changing the wording.

1. _____ The chef hardly uses any fat in his cooking.
2. __X__ I don't like no green peppers on my pizza.
3. __X__ I can barely see nothing anything in this fog.
4. _____ The instructions never say to use a hammer.
5. __X__ Nobody hardly showed up at the premier.
6. __X__ Nowhere does it say to not add butter.
7. __X__ Please do not assign no more homework.
8. _____ We can scarcely finish the work we have now.
9. __X__ They don't have no money left for the ride home.
10. _____ I want to go swimming on vacation, but not snorkeling.
11. __X__ He can't have no more cookies.
12. __X__ I don't want to go nowhere anywhere until I've finished my work.
13. __X__ She barely can find nothing without her glasses.
14. __X__ He can't never lift something that big.
15. _____ We won't plant these flowers until spring.

118

Rewrite It
As you rewrite the paragraph, correct the double negatives.

Firefighting is a brave and courageous job. If you can't imagine yourself not working hard, then this job isn't for you. Firefighters go through special training. They don't never take training lightly. Some trainees don't make it through this training. Firefighters must train in actual fires. They may find they don't like climbing no ladders that are so high. Some may find they aren't scarcely strong enough. The firefighters who graduate are ready for the job. They don't know nothing about what lies ahead, but they are trained and ready. Firefighters keep us, our pets, and our homes safe. Firefighting is a brave and courageous career to explore.

<u>Firefighting is a very brave and courageous job. If you can't imagine yourself working hard, then this job isn't for you. Firefighters go through special training. They never take training lightly. Firefighters must wear special gear and use special equipment. It isn't easy to use the equipment. They spend many class hours learning about it and training with it. Firefighters must train in actual fires. Some trainees don't make it through this training. They may find they don't like climbing ladders that are so high. Some may find they aren't strong enough. These men and women should still be respected for going through the training; it's just not the job for them. The firefighters who graduate are ready for the job. They don't know anything about what lies ahead, but they are trained and ready. Firefighters keep us, our pets, and our homes safe. Firefighting is a brave and courageous career to explore.</u>

Try It
Write four negative sentences using each of the following words: *not, nobody, nowhere,* and *nothing.* Do not use double negatives.

Answers will vary.

119

Synonyms are words that have the same, or almost the same, meaning. Using synonyms can help you avoid repeating words and can make your writing more interesting.
clever, smart   reply, answer   wreck, destroy   applaud, clap

Antonyms are words that have opposite meanings.
wide, narrow   accept, decline   break, repair   borrow, lend

Identify It
Read each sentence below. If the underlined words are synonyms, write **S** on the line. If they are antonyms, write **A** on the line.

1. ___A___ Do you know if the house at the end of the street is <u>vacant</u> or <u>occupied</u>?
2. ___S___ Although Tamika is <u>shy</u> now, I don't expect that she'll be <u>timid</u> her whole life.
3. ___S___ The hero of the story was <u>courageous</u>, and he was rewarded for being so <u>brave</u>.
4. ___A___ The plane <u>departs</u> at 11:00 and <u>arrives</u> at its destination at 2:30.
5. ___S___ The <u>commander</u> was well respected by his men, and they were happy to follow their <u>leader</u>.
6. ___A___ After visiting the <u>ancient</u> ruins, it seemed odd to return to our <u>modern</u> hotel.
7. ___A___ I'd like you to predict whether the water will <u>expand</u> or <u>contract</u> as it freezes.
8. ___S___ It has been <u>gusty</u> all morning, but I'm hoping it won't be so <u>windy</u> this afternoon.
9. ___S___ The <u>weary</u> traveler was too <u>exhausted</u> to continue along the trail.
10. ___A___ If you <u>fail</u> at something once, it doesn't mean you'll never <u>succeed</u>.

120

Complete It
Fill in each cloud with an antonym.

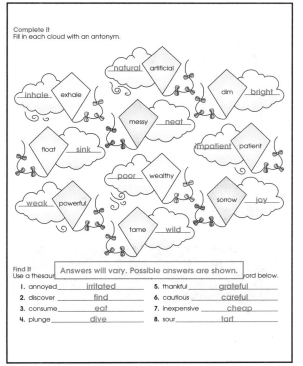

natural — artificial
inhale — exhale
dim — bright
messy — neat
float — sink
impatient — patient
poor — wealthy
weak — powerful
sorrow — joy
tame — wild

Find It
Use a thesaurus _____ word below.

Answers will vary. Possible answers are shown.

1. annoyed _____ irritated
2. discover _____ find
3. consume _____ eat
4. plunge _____ dive
5. thankful _____ grateful
6. cautious _____ careful
7. inexpensive _____ cheap
8. sour _____ tart

121

Homophones are words that sound the same but have different spellings and different meanings. There are hundreds of homophones in the English language.

Are you *allowed* to go to the midnight movie?
Practice saying your multiplication tables *aloud.*

Tomas *threw* the football to me.
The tunnel goes *through* the mountain.

If you are unsure about which homophone to use, look up the meanings in a dictionary.

Match It
Read the following sentences. Circle the letter of the definition of the underlined homophone that fits the sentence.

1. Taylor will have many books to <u>buy</u> when he starts college.
   (a.) to purchase
   b. to be near
2. The horse's <u>mane</u> glistened in the morning sunshine.
   a. the most important
   (b.) hair
3. My father said we weren't <u>allowed</u> to see that movie.
   (a.) to be permitted
   b. to be audible
4. Ellen lives <u>by</u> the pond with the ducks and geese.
   a. to purchase
   (b.) to be near
5. Please underline the sentence with the <u>main</u> idea in this paragraph.
   (a.) the most important
   b. hair
6. The students will recite the poems <u>aloud</u>.
   a. to be permitted
   (b.) to be audible

122

Page 123

Complete It

Complete the following sentences by circling the correct homophone in parentheses.

1. Today's lesson is about more than Presidents; it's about their pets, (to, **too**).

2. President Benjamin Harrison's grandchildren liked to hitch a small cart (**to**, too) the President's pet goat, His Whiskers, and ride around the White House lawn.

3. Once, His Whiskers escaped (threw, **through**) an open gate.

4. The President ran after His Whiskers and led the goat and the children back (**to**, too) the White House.

5. President Lyndon B. Johnson was kind (**to**, too) a stray when his daughter Luci found a small mutt.

6. President Calvin Coolidge's raccoon, Rebecca, had her own house on White House grounds. He walked (**to**, too) her house every day and took her on a walk on a leash.

7. Not only did Luci Johnson adopt a stray, but Chelsea Clinton, daughter of President Bill Clinton, did, (to, **too**).

8. When Chelsea went (**to**, too) college, the president's secretary, Betty Currie, took in Socks the cat.

9. The pets of (**passed**, past) Presidents are quite popular with the public.

Find It

Use a dictionary to ~~...~~ Write their definitions on the lines provided.

Answers will vary slightly. Accept all reasonable answers.

1. ad: __advertisement__
   add: __addition__
2. bail: __throw water out__
   bale: __bundle__
3. board: __lumber__
   bored: __uninterested__
4. bough: __of a tree__
   bow: __of a ship__
5. capital: __money; city__
   capitol: __U.S. Congress building__
6. do: __shall__
   dew: __moisture__
   due: __owed__
7. fair: __honest; bazaar__
   fare: __cost of transportation__
8. feat: __accomplishment__
   feet: __plural of *foot*__
9. flew: __past tense of *fly*__
   flu: __influenza__
   flue: __shaft__

123

Page 124

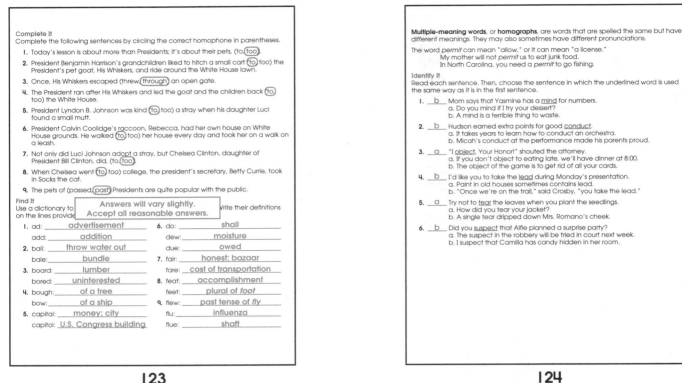

Multiple-meaning words, or **homographs**, are words that are spelled the same but have different meanings. They may also sometimes have different pronunciations.

The word *permit* can mean "allow," or it can mean "a license."
   My mother will not *permit* us to eat junk food.
   In North Carolina, you need a *permit* to go fishing.

Identify It

Read each sentence. Then, choose the sentence in which the underlined word is used the same way as it is in the first sentence.

1. __b__ Mom says that Yasmine has a <u>mind</u> for numbers.
   a. Do you mind if I try your dessert?
   b. A mind is a terrible thing to waste.

2. __b__ Hudson earned extra points for good <u>conduct</u>.
   a. It takes years to learn how to conduct an orchestra.
   b. Micah's conduct at the performance made his parents proud.

3. __a__ "I <u>object</u>, Your Honor!" shouted the attorney.
   a. If you don't object to eating late, we'll have dinner at 8:00.
   b. The object of the game is to get rid of all your cards.

4. __b__ I'd like you to take the <u>lead</u> during Monday's presentation.
   a. Paint in old houses sometimes contains lead.
   b. "Once we're on the trail," said Crosby, "you take the lead."

5. __a__ Try not to <u>tear</u> the leaves when you plant the seedlings.
   a. How did you tear your jacket?
   b. A single tear dripped down Mrs. Romano's cheek.

6. __b__ Did you <u>suspect</u> that Alfie planned a surprise party?
   a. The suspect in the robbery will be tried in court next week.
   b. I suspect that Camilla has candy hidden in her room.

124

Page 125

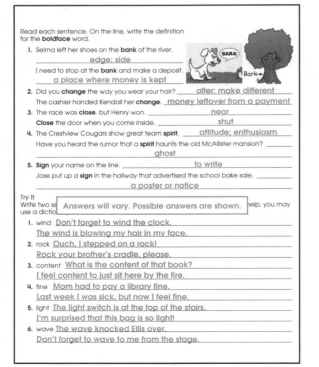

Read each sentence. On the line, write the definition for the **boldface** word.

1. Selma left her shoes on the **bank** of the river. __edge; side__
   I need to stop at the **bank** and make a deposit. __a place where money is kept__

2. Did you **change** the way you wear your hair? __alter; make different__
   The cashier handed Kendall her **change**. __money leftover from a payment__

3. The race was **close**, but Henry won. __near__
   Close the door when you come inside. __shut__

4. The Crestview Cougars show great team **spirit**. __attitude; enthusiasm__
   Have you heard the rumor that a **spirit** haunts the old McAllister mansion? __ghost__

5. **Sign** your name on the line. __to write__
   Jose put up a **sign** in the hallway that advertised the school bake sale. __a poster or notice__

Try It

Write two se~~...~~ *Answers will vary. Possible answers are shown.* help, you may use a dictio~~...~~

1. wind __Don't forget to wind the clock.__
   __The wind is blowing my hair in my face.__
2. rock __Ouch, I stepped on a rock!__
   __Rock your brother's cradle, please.__
3. content __What is the content of that book?__
   __I feel content to just sit here by the fire.__
4. fine __Mom had to pay a library fine.__
   __Last week I was sick, but now I feel fine.__
5. light __The light switch is at the top of the stairs.__
   __I'm surprised that this bag is so light!__
6. wave __The wave knocked Ellis over.__
   __Don't forget to wave to me from the stage.__

125

Page 126

A **simile** is a figure of speech that compares two things using the words *like* or *as*.
   Ansel slept *as soundly as a bear* in winter.
   The firecrackers boomed *like thunder* across the sky.

A **metaphor** is a figure of speech that compares two unlike things that are similar in some way.
   The grass was a cool carpet beneath Marisa's feet.
   Aunt Hattie was a mama bear when it came to protecting her children.

Similes and metaphors make writing more interesting and vivid for the reader.

Identify It

Read each sentence below. On the line, write **S** if it contains a simile and **M** if it contains a metaphor.

1. __M__ The full moon was a plump, friendly face peeking over the hill.
2. __M__ In the middle of rush hour, the highway was a parking lot.
3. __S__ Chase was excited to go, but his brother moved as slowly as molasses.
4. __S__ The hail felt like tiny stinging bees as it pelted my skin.
5. __M__ Rico is a night owl—he rarely goes to bed before midnight.
6. __S__ The wildflowers by the side of the road were as colorful as a bag of confetti thrown into the air.
7. __M__ The skater was a graceful swan as she glided across the ice.
8. __S__ In the sunlight, the creek sparkled like stars in the night sky.
9. __S__ The dinosaur's teeth shone like rows of small white daggers.
10. __M__ Jazmin is a walking dictionary—she has an amazing vocabulary.

126

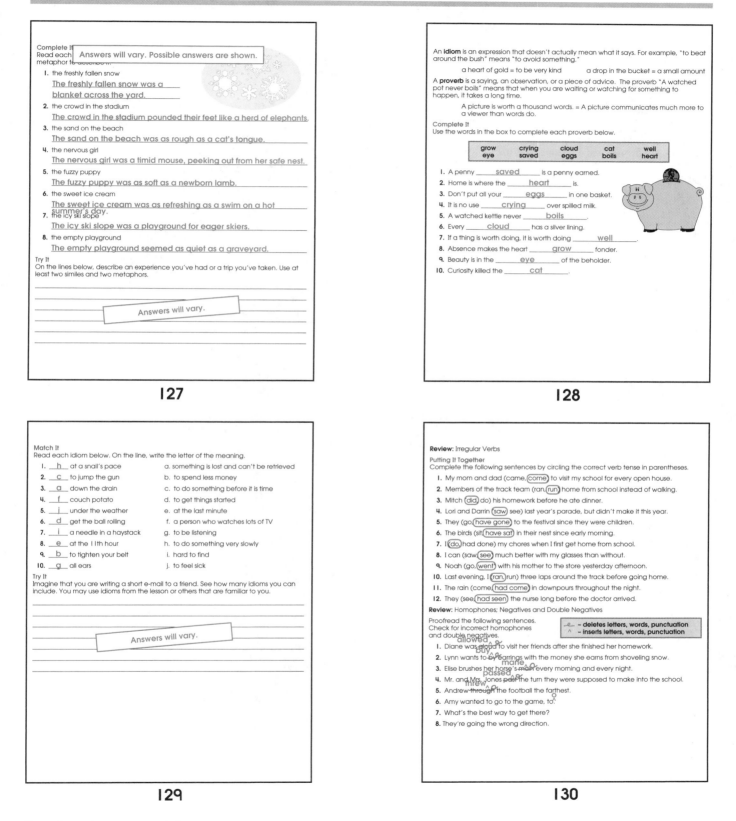

Complete It
Read each [Answers will vary. Possible answers are shown.]
metaphor to describe it.

1. the freshly fallen snow

   The freshly fallen snow was a
   blanket across the yard.

2. the crowd in the stadium

   The crowd in the stadium pounded their feet like a herd of elephants.

3. the sand on the beach

   The sand on the beach was as rough as a cat's tongue.

4. the nervous girl

   The nervous girl was a timid mouse, peeking out from her safe nest.

5. the fuzzy puppy

   The fuzzy puppy was as soft as a newborn lamb.

6. the sweet ice cream

   The sweet ice cream was as refreshing as a swim on a hot summer's day.

7. the icy ski slope

   The icy ski slope was a playground for eager skiers.

8. the empty playground

   The empty playground seemed as quiet as a graveyard.

Try It
On the lines below, describe an experience you've had or a trip you've taken. Use at least two similes and two metaphors.

Answers will vary.

127

An **idiom** is an expression that doesn't actually mean what it says. For example, "to beat around the bush" means "to avoid something."

    a heart of gold = to be very kind   a drop in the bucket = a small amount

A **proverb** is a saying, an observation, or a piece of advice. The proverb "A watched pot never boils" means that when you are waiting or watching for something to happen, it takes a long time.

    A picture is worth a thousand words. = A picture communicates much more to a viewer than words do.

Complete It
Use the words in the box to complete each proverb below.

grow	crying	cloud	cat	well
eye	saved	eggs	boils	heart

1. A penny _____saved_____ is a penny earned.
2. Home is where the _____heart_____ is.
3. Don't put all your _____eggs_____ in one basket.
4. It is no use _____crying_____ over spilled milk.
5. A watched kettle never _____boils_____.
6. Every _____cloud_____ has a silver lining.
7. If a thing is worth doing, it is worth doing _____well_____.
8. Absence makes the heart _____grow_____ fonder.
9. Beauty is in the _____eye_____ of the beholder.
10. Curiosity killed the _____cat_____.

128

Match It
Read each idiom below. On the line, write the letter of the meaning.

1. __h__ at a snail's pace   a. something is lost and can't be retrieved
2. __c__ to jump the gun   b. to spend less money
3. __a__ down the drain   c. to do something before it is time
4. __f__ couch potato   d. to get things started
5. __j__ under the weather   e. at the last minute
6. __d__ get the ball rolling   f. a person who watches lots of TV
7. __i__ a needle in a haystack   g. to be listening
8. __e__ at the 11th hour   h. to do something very slowly
9. __b__ to tighten your belt   i. hard to find
10. __g__ all ears   j. to feel sick

Try It
Imagine that you are writing a short e-mail to a friend. See how many idioms you can include. You may use idioms from the lesson or others that are familiar to you.

Answers will vary.

129

Review: Irregular Verbs

Putting It Together
Complete the following sentences by circling the correct verb tense in parentheses.

1. My mom and dad (came, come) to visit my school for every open house.
2. Members of the track team (ran, run) home from school instead of walking.
3. Mitch (did, do) his homework before he ate dinner.
4. Lori and Darrin (saw, see) last year's parade, but didn't make it this year.
5. They (go, have gone) to the festival since they were children.
6. The birds (sit, have sat) in their nest since early morning.
7. I (do, had done) my chores when I first get home from school.
8. I can (saw, see) much better with my glasses than without.
9. Noah (go, went) with his mother to the store yesterday afternoon.
10. Last evening, I (ran, run) three laps around the track before going home.
11. The rain (come, had come) in downpours throughout the night.
12. They (see, had seen) the nurse long before the doctor arrived.

Review: Homophones; Negatives and Double Negatives

Proofread the following sentences.
Check for incorrect homophones
and double negatives.

| ~~e~~ – deletes letters, words, punctuation |
| ^ – inserts letters, words, punctuation |

1. Diane was ~~aloud~~ allowed to visit her friends after she finished her homework.
2. Lynn wants to ~~by~~ buy earrings with the money she earns from shoveling snow.
3. Elise brushes her horse's ~~main~~ mane every morning and every night.
4. Mr. and Mrs. Jones ~~past~~ passed the turn they were supposed to make into the school.
5. Andrew ~~through~~ threw the football the farthest.
6. Amy wanted to go to the game, to.~~o~~
7. What's the best way to get there?
8. They're going the wrong direction.

130

Review: Comparative and Superlative Adjectives

Identify the correct use of adjectives and adverbs by circling the correct answer in parentheses.

1. Stephanie thought "The Wizard of Oz" was the (cute, (cutest)) play she had seen all year.
2. We have to climb over one ((big,) biggest) rock in order to pass the test.
3. That is the (bigger, (biggest)) mountain I've ever seen.
4. Clint makes ((more,) most) money mowing lawns than Perry does selling lemonade.
5. The ice storm we had last night was ((worse,) worst) than the one we had last year.
6. The blizzard brought the (more, (most)) snow I had ever seen.
7. I think swimming in the lake in the winter is a ((bad,) badly) idea.

Review: Synonyms, Antonyms, and Multiple-Meaning Words

In each sentence below, a pair of words is underlined. On the line, write **S** if the words are synonyms, **A** if they are antonyms, or **M** if they are multiple-meaning words.

1. __A__ Do you store your summer clothes in the <u>attic</u> or the <u>basement</u>?
2. __M__ Be careful that when you <u>bow</u>, your <u>bow</u> doesn't slip out of your hair.
3. __S__ The <u>presents</u> are on the table, and the guests can't wait for you to open your <u>gifts</u>.
4. __S__ Did Rascal <u>eat</u> the entire bone, or did he <u>consume</u> only part of it?
5. __A__ That bread is <u>stale</u>, but I did make some <u>fresh</u> bread today.
6. __M__ Mom put Clare's <u>down</u> comforter <u>down</u> the laundry chute.

131